The Contemporary Contrabass

THE NEW INSTRUMENTATION

Editors

Bertram Turetzky & Barney Childs

Executive Editor
University of California Press

Alain Hénon

1. Bertram Turetzky, THE CONTEMPORARY CONTRABASS

2. Thomas Howell, THE AVANT-GARDE FLUTE: A HANDBOOK FOR COMPOSERS

AND, FLUTISTS

The Contemporary Contrabass

BERTRAM TURETZKY

UNIVERSITY OF CALIFORNIA PRESS

Berkeley · Los Angeles · London · 1974

University of California Press

Berkeley and Los Angeles, California

University of California Press, Ltd.

London, England

This book is dedicated to the memory of my father

ISADORE TURETZKY

1904 - 1973

Preface

Perhaps the most important purpose of this book is to articulate the real musical image and potential of the noble, misunderstood contrabass. The instrument's image in concert halls is still exemplified by Saint-Saens "L'Elephant," with its satirical quotations from Mendelssohn's "Midsummer Night's Dream" and Berlioz's "Ballet des Sylphes." This musical joke has been made at the expense of the instrument that performs it. It has perpetuated the myth that "the doublebass from its very nature — its tone when heard alone being somewhat rough, and its treatment owing to its large dimensions, very difficult — is essentially an orchestral instrument rather than a soloist."

This myth has been dispelled certainly by the solo efforts of such artists as Jimmy Blanton, David Walter, Charles Mingus, Gary Karr, Scott LaFaro, and others; yet the instrument has not been written about or discussed intelligently in orchestration books or other books, or on film, TV, videotape, etc., the only exception being the three books of Raymond Elgar.

The contrabass lives in limbo in most American music schools, since it isn't really accepted in the string department (where it belongs) and is usually considered an adjunct of the orchestral instruments department. Some of these hallowed institutions that do offer a contrabass degree do not even require recitals! A perusal of the contests for young instrumentalists reveals that the contrabass is not included much of the time, even when they say "string instruments." This situation was and continues to be intolerable!

In the early 1950's, long before militant activists were au courant, I committed myself to work toward changing the public and professional image of the contrabass. In order to do this, I realized that concertizing was the key, which in the 1950's was impossible mainly because of the lack of literature available. I attacked this problem in two directions:

1. locating original contrabass music from the eighteenth and nineteenth centuries, and
2. commissioning twentieth century music.

After five years of research, I unearthed a good deal of solo and chamber music for category (1), most of which did not merit excavation. The search for music of our time brought some results, mostly cello=conceived compositions transcribed "an octave lower and slower." This period was closed in 1959 when I began to write composers throughout the country for music for contrabass. If they hadn't written solo or chamber music for the instrument I asked whether they would consider it. Many pieces came in and my career in the concert hall began. Since then approximately 150 pieces have been written for me, more than doubling the original literature I knew as a young student in the early 1950's. In order to have accomplished this without foundation money for my commissions, as I did and still do, the composers had to hear something special in the demonstrations I played or taped for them, and I had to perform the works. These last two requirements put the pressure on, and besides learning how to be a concert artist and concert manager I had to look into the instrument and be able to show composers what was special about the contrabass. This is the genesis of my timbral research.

At the end of my first decade of work in this area I feel that a study of the history of Western string playing points out that from the earliest times performers and composers were much concerned with tone color. For example, in the first printed viol method by Sylvestro di Ganassi, Regola Rubertin (1542 and 1543), we find an exposition of registration. Playing sul tasto will produce sad effects and the area near the bridge is to be used for stronger and harsher sounds. The middle of the space between the bridge and the end of the fingerboard was recommended as the normal playing area and it still is, unless some insensitive or unschooled string player uses it for sul tasto or sul ponticello.

Documented evidence is readily available to substantiate the concept that viol technique, complete with its arsenal of sounds and "bag of tricks," was taken into the "new" technique of the violin. More than documentation for the above is found in Farina's Capriccio Stravagante No. 27 where glissando, col legno, and sul ponticello are used to portray barking dogs, yowling cats, and crowing cocks!

On into the seventeenth and early eighteenth century we still find timbre a prime concern. When the short-necked violin goes out, the bass bar comes in, etc. The aesthetic of "bel canto" takes over on two levels: (1) tone quality or beauty, and (2) power (projection).

These aspects of string playing are vital to the development of the aesthetics of string playing until the late nineteenth century, when sound becomes an end in itself. The twentieth century is slowly beginning to see the dangers of the worship of sound and I see a circular movement back to the earlier concepts of Western instruments and further back to the very wellsprings of stringed instruments — the East. A great deal of work is going to be done in this area. What an image in the mind's eye when we think of the sarangi — "The Voice of a Hundred Colors!"

The contrabass is the only orchestral instrument in Western art music that comes in two varieties —

1. The solo bass is a smaller instrument, ranging from a mensur of 39 1/2 to 41 1/2 inches, usually tuned A, E, B, F♯. It possesses a light cello-type sound.

2. The orchestra bass is a powerful instrument with a rich, dark sound and a mensur of 41 1/2 to 46 inches, tuned G, D, A, E. Often the five string (G, D, A, E, C) is used, or an extension is added to the four string model.

Despite the enormous difference between these two instruments, few if any orchestration books in English have ever discussed this very basic and significant fact. The first track on the accompanying LP will illuminate this difference in sound.

This book is not concerned with presenting an exhaustive inventory of the contrabass potential but hopes to introduce some new concepts, aesthetics, and techniques to composers and performers.

I have avoided categorizing the technical difficulties of many of these ideas as they are new and not yet in the mainstream of performance and pedagogy. Further, the reader will note that a section on notation, which some of my composer/consultants have suggested, is not included. It is my feeling that the time between this printing and the second edition will suffice to suggest and select the best notational concepts from a more substantial literature than we possess now.

My dear friend Barney Childs, who edited this book, has always generously found time, over the past decade, from a busy composing and teaching schedule to write music for me as well as discuss, advise, debate, encourage, and assist me with my writing. I feel privileged to have such a friend.

Another dear friend and noted composer, Donald Erb, has collaborated often with me over the last ten years. Our numerous discussions of aesthetics and timbre have inspired much of this book.

I feel unusually fortunate to have as colleagues such excellent composers as Robert Erickson and Kenneth Gaburo, both of whom have collaborated with me since the early 1960's and helped to inspire this work. They have been readers, contributors, and critics for various sections of this book.

Many of America's finest contrabassists have found time in their busy schedules to answer my letters. I should like to extend my thanks to:

Jon Deak	New York Philharmonic
Murray Grodner	University of Indiana
Bob Gladstone	Detroit Symphony
Larry Hurst	University of Michigan

Edward Krolick	University of Illinois
Gary Karr	Yale University
Peter Mecurio	UCLA
Eldon Obrecht	University of Iowa
Henry Portnoi	Boston Symphony
Roger Scott	Philadelphia Orchestra

David Walter (Julliard and Manhattan School of Music), the late Frederick Zimmerman (Julliard and New York Philharmonic), and Warren Benfield (Chicago Symphony and Northwestern University) have made significant contributions in the many conversations and letters our hectic schedules allowed us to arrange during the last decade. The gracious encouragement of these distinguished artists and pedagogues has lit the way in many dark hours.

To the large list of composer friends who have sent "feedback" after receiving certain chapters, an enormous debt of gratitude:

Paul Chihara	Richard Moryl
George Crumb	Will Ogdon
Ingolf Dahl	Pauline Oliveros
Edward Diemente	George Rochberg
Jacob Druckman	Griffith Rose
Steve Fisher	William Sydeman
Sydney Hodkinson	Richard Wernick
Ernst Krenek	Charles Whittenberg
Eugene Kurtz	Jogi Yuasa
Donald Martino	

I should like to extend appreciation also to the many composers and publishers for the rights to include the musical examples in this book: to McGinnis & Marx Music Publishers, for Barney Childs, Sonata for Bass Alone, Copyright 1960, Josef Marx; and William Sydeman, For Double Bass Alone, Copyright 1959, Josef Marx; to Media Press, for Jon Deak, Color Studies for Contrabass, © Copyright Media Press, Champaign, Illinois, 1969, All Rights Reserved; to E.C. Schirmer Music Company, for Richard Felciano, Spectra, © Copyright 1971 by E.C. Schirmer Music Co.; to C.F. Peters Corporation, for Stephen Fisher, Concert Piece, Copyright © 1968 by C.F. Peters Corp.; Paul Chihara, Logs (copyright transferred in 1970 to Henmar Press, Inc.); C. Whittenberg, Conversations, © 1968 by C.F. Peters Corp.; and Lou Harrison, Suite, Copyright © 1961 by C.F. Peters Corp.

To David Cope, editor of the Composer, I owe many thanks for his encouragement, suggestions, and help in getting Chapters III and IV into print.

The calligraphy of Donald Balestieri and Loretta Kirkell has brought grace and clarity to the visual parameters of this book and I am forever grateful.

Special thanks go to three talented young musicians, currently graduate students at UCSD, who have assisted in a variety of ways — the composers Frank McCarty and Allen Strange, and percussionist John Grimes.

Samuel Kolstein, master Luthier, has given generously of his time and knowledge over the last decade, and taught me much about instruments, their adjustment and setup.

The kindness and patience of my editor, Alain Hénon, has helped maintain the level of energy originally committed to this book and has been a beacon during the long night of its birth.

Much of this book was written during the summers, and I received support from the research committee of UCSD. I owe much to the enlightened administrative policies at my university which made much of the preliminary research possible and which freed time for me during those three summers. I owe thanks for typing and secretarial help to Miss Bonnie Barnett and, especially, my wife Nancy.

Chapter I grew out of an article I wrote in 1967 for my recording The New World of Sound (Ars Nova Records), and was expanded and developed under a research grant from the Academic Senate of UCSD in the summer of 1969.

Chapter II grew out of a series of lectures I gave in 1969-1970 in Robert Erickson's Instrumentation class at UCSD. A research grant took me across the country in the summer of 1970 for consultation with colleagues and the chapter was completed in October of 1970.

Chapter III is a revised and expanded version of an article, "The Bass as a Drum," first printed in The Composer (Sept. 1969) and reprinted in the Bass Sound Post (Dec. 1969). It is used here with the permission of the editors.

Chapter IV was originally an article, "Vocal and Speech Sounds — A Technique of Contemporary Writing for the Contrabass," first published in The Composer (Winter, 1969) and later reprinted in the Bass Sound Post. It is reprinted here with the permission of the editors.

Chapter V has been the favorite seminar topic in my touring of the last decade and one of the consistently problematical aspects of modern music performance.

Chapter VI had its inception in a lecture given to the American Society of University Composers Fourth National Conference at UCSB in March 1969. It has developed through the last three years of touring the country in lecture recitals and research.

Chapter VII was written for this book by Mr. Arnold Lazarus, a physicist/musician who has done some of the outstanding work in this field.

Please note that the technical information in this book is derived from my work with a standard-sized contrabass, set up with steel strings tuned orchestrally (G, D, A, E).

Some of these ideas may not work for a larger instrument or one set up with gut strings. Also, finally, the thrust of this book is toward solo and chamber music composition and performance, not orchestral music.

If, after reading this book, more composers begin to cultivate compositions for the contrabass and performers reevaluate their approach, my efforts will be more than rewarded.

Bertram Turetzky
Del Mar, California

Contents

Chapter I: Pizzicato

The starting point of this work is a reevaluation of pizzicato technique, until recently a barren wasteland in Western art music with the exception of some isolated moments in orchestral, chamber, and solo scores by Paganini, Elgar, Tchaikowsky, and Bartok.

Apparently little or no heed was paid to Berlioz when he suggested that string players should study pizzicato in order to have more velocity and agility:

> The study of the violin is incomplete. Pupils are not taught pizzicato. As a result a whole host of passages in arpeggios involving all four strings, or in repeated notes with two or three fingers on the same string in rapid tempo — passages which are perfectly feasible, as any guitar player will show you (on the violin) — are said to be impossible and consequently proscribed to composers. No doubt fifty years from now a director with a flair for innovation will take the plunge and lay it down that pizzicato is to be taught in violin classes; and then violinists, having mastered the novel and piquant effects that are possible with this technique, will laugh at our present-day players, just as ours now laugh at the fiddlers of the last century, with their cautionary "Watch out for the C!" and with reason. [1]

In jazz, I found a solo pizzicato tradition of over half a century, so I began to research this area in the 1950's. It was immediately clear that the work of Jimmy Blanton (d. 1942), Oscar Pettiford, Charles Mingus, Scott La Faro (d. 1961), Richard Davis, Gary Peacock, and Ray Brown had much to offer so-called legit technique. In fact, the standard pizzicato technique of younger bassists all over the world has been reenergized by the jazz experience. It would seem that a culmination was reached in the work of La Faro, who had developed a 2-4 finger technique with the clarity of a guitarist. Conceptually, enormous changes were brought about, but it is the agility, accuracy, and velocity that concerned me. Clearly, my direction was not toward more speed but toward new vistas of timbre.

---

[1] Hector Berlioz, The Memoirs of Hector Berlioz, trans. David Cairno (London: Victor Gollanez, Ltd., 1969), p. 401. (Fifth letter to Humbert Ferrand, from Prague.)

GENERATORS

The traditional European "legitimate" pizzicato technique was a first or double first and second finger style, plucking straight across the fleshy part of the fingertip.[2] Many of the jazz players preferred the slightly angled one-finger style, with the thumb often under the fingerboard acting as a fulcrum. Another style, the two fingers or finger-over-finger style, became more in vogue in the 1950's because it offered the player greater clarity and velocity. It is now "stock in trade" for the younger players, but was, curiously enough, mentioned in Monteverdi's Il Combattimento di Tancredi e Clorinda (1627) and also in the bible of the German school of bass playing, Franz Simandl's celebrated method of about 1869.[3] Some players utilize all the fingers for a full-bodied pizzicato sound. Most bassists use this technique for the slap pizzicato,[4] which has, during the last decade, been referred to as the Bartok pizzicato. From the temporal vantage point of the 1970's, the clearest term is "slap pizzicato." So from here on the term "slap pizzicato" will be used to translate the symbol ♂ and the sound of the string hitting the fingerboard.

Besides the traditional use of fingers 1, 2, 3, and 4, the thumb is also an important generator of pizzicato technique. I found in the late 1950's that by using my thumb as a plectrum, a dark, sustained quasi-guitar sound, which lent itself uniquely to lyric writing, was produced. The earliest, most significant employment of the technique is found in Monody II for Solo Double Bass (1962) by George Perle:[5]

---

[2] Simandl, New Method for the Double Bass, ed. Fred Zimmerman (New York: Carl Fischer, Inc., 1954), p. 79. The strings are picked in the direction from left ro right. In piano and Mezzo-forte passages, either the fore or middle finger may be used; but for forte passages, both are employed."

[3] Ibid. Simandl said, "For pizzicato passages in quick tempo, the fore and middle fingers should be employed alternately."

[4] Ibid. "When making contact with the string the right hand raises the string from the fingerboard and then lets it strike the wood. A violent, vibrant sound is produced. This technique is probably the best known of the many percussion sounds possible on string instruments."

[5] Recorded by the author on Advance Recordings: A Recital of New Music, Bertram Turetzky, double bass, 1964.

Example 1: Monody II for Solo Double Bass (1962), George Perle

Listening to the composer's demonstrations of this technique recorded at the time, I realize that I was attempting to emulate two of my musical heroes, lutenist Joseph Iadone and guitarist Andrés Segovia. The conscious study of Eastern and Western plucked string instruments then was the driving force behind this development, though some instrumentalists, such as Lunsford Morris "Corde" Corzine, advocated the use of thumb pizzicato[6] with advantages including articulation, projection, and velocity, as well as clarity of pitch. [7]

Thumb Pizzicato. Of necessity I have developed the "thumb pizzicato" and subsequently discovered that it gives FASTER changes from Arco to Pizzicato and Pizzicato to Arco. (See diagram below.)
The thumb pizzicato occurs in the opposite direction from the finger pizzicato. It is a push and that describes what it does — it gives a LIFT to the orchestra. It takes place on the upper part of the string, instead of the lower, thus producing clear tones in all degrees of dynamics, from finest PP to strongest FF, never a "slap" or "boom."
Experience in orchestral and solo performance, in Europe and the USA, in Symphony, Opera, Ballet, Musical Comedy, and Dance playing has proven this "thumb pizzicato" is of extraordinary value, due to its pure sounding of true notes provided on the upper string, clear as bell notes, never fuzzy. With my "thumb pizzicato" 16ths and 32nds are not skipped, they sound precisely rhythmical. Thus no missed notes, in changes from Pizz. to Arco and Arco to Pizz. Having worked the problem out as a result of playing string bass with classicists and modernists such as Leopold Stokowski, Efrem Kurtz, Adolph Busch, Martha Graham (to mention a few), in Musical Comedy, i.e., Brigadoon, Miss Liberty, where this is solving many problems in the stream of versatility required by the baton of Jay Blackton, I commend this to the advancement of string bass playing. [8]

---

[6] It is interesting to note that Berlioz prescribes guitar pizzicato in the Damnation of Faust (1846); in the solo of Mephistopheles the second violins and viola are directed to use the thumb for their four=note chords.

[7] In his preface to Findiesen's Complete Method for String Bass (New York: M. Baron Co., 1947).

[8] Corzine, in the preface to Findiesen.

Example 2: Thumb Pizzicato (2 movements)

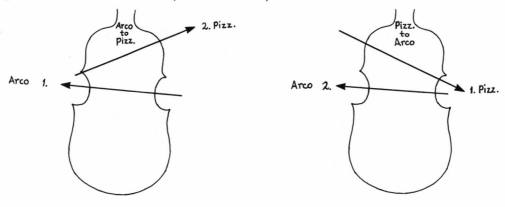

Example 3: Finger Style (3 movements)

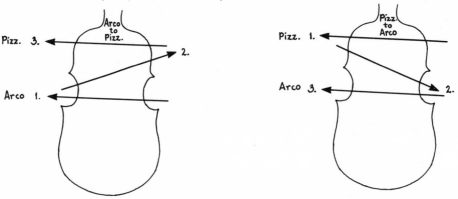

My direction was thus a personal, not a universal feeling (i.e., interpretation) of this technique. The thumb pizzicato has been named "guitar pizzicato" because of its lack of pretense and because it best describes the sound produced. The next use of guitar pizzicato known to me is found in George Crumb's Three Madrigals for Soprano, Vibraphone and Contrabass (1965) (see Example 4 below). The guitarlike "sound ideal" was in the air, and Crumb uses the technique chordally as opposed to the linear approach of Perle.

Example 4: Three Madrigals for Soprano, Vibraphone and Contrabass (1965),
George Crumb

      III. Los Muertos Llevan alas de musgo

           (The dead wear mossy wings) quasi una chitarra bassa

The fingernail is another generator and is excellent for short sounds at a low to medium dynamic level.[9]   Finally, a regular Spanish guitar plectrum (tortoise shell or plastic) and finger picks (shell, plastic, or metal) show an enormous potential.[10] The regular plectrum has been used in a most colorful instance in this musical example by Barney Childs:

Example 5: <u>Mr. T., His Fancy</u> (1967)[11]

LYRIC PIZZICATO

Everyday pizzicato=playing on all the string instruments in orchestral and chamber music is not only colorless but, usually, <u>non espressivo.</u> More enterprising composers and conductors are calling for greater differentiation between short and long, as well as the standard timbral differentiations. Hard to believe, but true, is that one had to wait until 1960 to find a composition that differentiated between <u>non espressivo</u> pizzicato and a more lyric <u>pizzicato espressivo.</u> This work is Barney Childs' <u>Sonata for Bass Alone</u> (1960). At the beginning of the second movement the composer indicates "pizzicato sempre, swing easy" and calls for a mellow, full sound without vibrato and with much forward motion, i.e., drive. In the middle section, Childs calls for "legit. legato." The concept of writing lyric pizzicato music was (in 1960) and still is (in 1970) visionary. Childs has opened an area that merits further investigation and use.

---

[9] Bernard Rogers mentions fingernail pizzicato on p. 17 of his <u>The Art of Orchestration</u> (New York: Appleton-Century Crofts, 1951).

[10] The quasi-banjo picking style adopted by Steve Swallow on "I Want You," a Bob Dylan song recorded with Gary Burton on the RCA Victor label, <u>Gary Burton Quartet in Concert</u>, LSP 3985, reinforces this idea conclusively.

[11] Recorded by Bertram Turetzky on ARS Nova Records: "The New World of Sound" (1967).

Example 6: Sonata for Bass Alone (1960), Barney Childs

Movement II

Very freely shape each phrase

REGISTRATION

When most string players put down the bow to play pizzicato, they invariably turn off their sensitivity to color, forgetting that pizzicato technique includes the same registration possibilities as bowing technique.   Therefore, pizzicato can and must be sul tasto, normale, and sul ponticello. [12] These distinctively different colors most definitely exist. Registration, especially in pizzicato playing, became a feature of my demonstrations and lectures in the late 1950's and is rapidly appearing in the repertoire.   Richard Felciano makes imaginative use of registration in the following example from Spectra (1966): [13]

Example 7: Spectra (1966), Richard Felciano

SLURRED PIZZICATO

In passages where the composer desires to approximate the legato sound of several notes played in one bow, slurred pizzicato is employed. A slur over the notes to be connected and sounded with only one impulse (pluck) will relay this information to the performer.

Example 8:

---

[12] Bernard Rogers suggests pizzicato sul ponticello in The Art of Orchestration, p. 20.

[13] Recorded by the Turetzkys on Ars Nova Recording AN-1008.

The slurred notes should be available in one hand position so as to be playable without shifting. A two or three note motif should be within the range of a major second or minor third. A four note motif should consist of minor seconds within the range of a minor or a major third. Slurred pizzicati are often used by jazz bassists to play passages that would be unplayable had they to articulate each note with a pizzicato.

This next passage is playable either one pizzicato to a note or slurred. The composer added the slur to facilitate its articulation for performers who were without formidable pizzicato technique.

Example 9: Piece for Four (1966), Olly Wilson [14]

Movement one

PIZZICATO TREMOLO

The pizzicato tremolo,[15] which is reminiscent of the second of such plectrum instruments as the oud, bouzouki, and Spanish guitar, came from research with the two-fingered jazz pizzicato technique. The first appearance of the technique is briefly found in the cadenza of the Elgar violin concerto of 1910. In his Ricercar á 3 (1967),[16] Robert Erickson makes monumental use of this technique in both lyrical expressive (Ex. 10) and bravura coloristic (Ex. 11) passagework.

Example 10: Ricercar á 3 (1967), Robert Erickson

espr. rich

---

[14] Recorded by the author, R. Willoughby (flute), L. Young (trumpet), and J. Schwartz, for CRI, SD264.

[15] Let's be clear about pizzicato tremolo, and its introduction into the new literature. The idea was "in the air" since 1910 and was used occasionally by jazz players also. My point is that I felt this technique had a tremendous potential and I made it a focal point in lectures, demonstrations, and improvizations. Bernard Rogers refers to pizzicato tremolo (The Art of Orchestration) as bisbigliando, but I prefer not to crib from harp terminology.

[16] Recorded by the author on Ars Nova Records (1967).

Example 11: <u>Ricercar á 3</u> (1967), Robert Erickson

LEFT HAND ALONE

This technique calls for a strong left hand articulation or "finger slap" that produces a mix of pizzicatolike sound and percussion ("finger slap" against the fingerboard). [17] Its first appearance in printed music is found in the <u>Monody II</u> (1962) by George Perle. In 1963 Thomas Frederickson made prophetic use of the technique in his <u>Music for the Double Bass Alone</u> (Ex. 12).

Example 12: <u>Music for the Double Bass Alone</u> (1963), Thomas Frederickson

Frederickson's pairing of a melodic line, played left hand alone, accompanied by a pizzicato tremolo drone, produced a two-part texture with the sound of sitar and tambura. It is Robert Erickson who brings this technique into the literature in complete fruition.   The fusion with guitar pizzicato, pizzicato tremolo, glissando, and left hand alone brought about by Erickson will firmly establish the lyric pizzicato technique as a basic and important aspect of the contrabass idiomatic potential.

---

[17] This is a natural sound to fuse or contrast with pizzicato and col legno. In fact, it is so natural that it hasn't been done!

TWO-HANDED PIZZICATO

Two-handed pizzicato, an extension of the left hand alone technique, offers composer and performer another possibility of using two voices. It is a new area with no printed example known to me, and since it is in the laboratory phase I should like to suggest the following:

1. Write slow parts as the right hand is not as strong or accurate as the left hand and time must be spent practicing and developing strength and agility.

2. The first or first and second fingers used in conjunction would be the generators.

3. Difficulty in coordinating the two parts should be avoided until (1) is solved.

BI-TONES

The bi-tone is often a by-product of left hand alone technique. It occurs when both halves of the string are activated. [18] Most instruments produce bi-tones (with left hand alone) inadvertently on the first and second strings (sometimes the third string also) after the minor sixth. Bi-tones can also be produced by a two-finger pizzicato, with one finger on each side of the finger stopping the string. Thus the tones can be short or long (pizzicato tremolo) and soft (left hand alone) or moderately loud (pizzicato tremolo) but can only be sounded left hand alone or pizzicato. [19]

Example 13: "Thick Purple" from <u>Color Studies for Contrabass</u> (1969), Jon Deak

The only printed examples of this technique are found in works of Jon Deak and Kenneth Gaburo. The first example consists of bowing one side of the string and plucking the other.

---

[18] The bassist must dampen one end of the string in order to eliminate the resultant bi-tones, if so desired.

[19] Jon Deak, in his <u>Color Studies</u> (1969), calls for the bow on the "other side," but since these pitches are available in "home turf" it seems senseless to get rosin caked on your strings in the lower positions. The only justification would be a visual/theatrical one — out of the range of this work.

Example 14: "Woman and Bird before the Moon" from <u>Surrealist Studies</u> (1970), Jon Deak

An audible two-way glissando is possible when using the two-fingered pizzicato tremolo (see Plate 1). This seemingly impossible audio hallucination is used for the first time in printed music, with great imagination, by Kenneth Gaburo in <u>Inside</u> (1969). He uses it in three parts with a vocal glissando added as well as in the original form. Gaburo's notation is very clear and is presented in the next example.

Example 15: <u>Inside</u> (1969), Kenneth Gaburo

The interest in bi-tone technique in lectures and recitals during the past few years has been very intense and gratifying. Many questions have been asked about the history and development of this technique. I am indebted to John Grimes whose industrious research on the Futurists has unearthed the only information known at this writing. This self-explanatory document, printed in translation, will clearly establish the bi-tone genesis and is found in the Appendix.

<u>LEFT HAND PIZZICATO</u>

Left hand pizzicato is used in three different ways:

1. One finger stops the string or gets a harmonic, while another (l.h.) finger "plucks" the string. Left hand pizzicati are normally designated by a "+" (see Ex. 16).

2. Left hand pizzicati are often used to reinforce arco sounds (see Ex. 17).

3. Left hand pizzicato can be used to create another line (see Ex. 18).

Example 16:

Example 17:

Example 18: <u>For Double Bass Alone</u> (1959), William Sydeman[20]

Use of the other side of the string plucked with a left hand finger produces a reverse left hand pizzicato.

Example 19: "Fog White," from Color Studies for Contrabass (1969), Jon Deak

DOUBLE STOPS

This discussion has been limited primarily to pizzicato technique in relation to single pitches. The next two examples are of pizzicato octaves, introduced into the printed literature by William Sydeman in 1959.

---

[20] Recorded by the author for Advance Records (1964).

Example 20: <u>For Double Bass Alone</u> (1959), William Sydeman

Movement II

This technique is rather idiomatic, and octaves over the full range are possible. At about the fifth position octaves become very comfortable. This area of double stops on nonadjacent strings is still (in 1970) a lacuna. The following examples show the possibilities of double stops played pizzicato on nonadjacent strings, i.e., I-III, or II-IV. Double stops on I-IV are available played pizzicato and feasible up to the seventh position. After this point, the problem of strength to press down the E string makes it an individual problem.

Example 21: Double stops on I-III

Example 22: Double stops on II-IV

TRIPLE STOPS

The triple stop potential is enormous when one considers the possible string combinations: I-II-III; I-II-IV; II-III-IV. Multiple stops are awesome difficulty to begin with, and the difference in size and strength of the performers' hands compounds the problem. At this stage, composers should consult with the individual performer. It is my hope that triple and quadruple stops find their way into the literature, since the next step is into the world of pedagogy and the mainstream of performance.

A most extensive and outstanding use of multiple stops is found in the large-scaled Sonata for String Bass (1964) by Peter Phillips.[21]   A guitar sound was desired, calling for enormous digital strength to produce the chords with the necessary ease and fluidity.

Example 23: Sonata for String Bass (1964), Peter Phillips

To conclude this section I must say that the physical problems — time needed to set the hand, agility, and accuracy — are all individual performance problems and universals cannot be set at this stage of the development of the new technique.

CODA

(Coda sections contain recent material not yet incorporated into the text.)

1. A buzz can be achieved when a string already activated is touched lightly by a fingernail (l.h. usually). This is found in Valentine (1969) by Jacob Druckman and in numerous scores of John Cage.

2. Pizzicato behind the bridge produces harplike tones as well as a visual dimension (that can vary from grace to hysteria).

3. Very high pizzicato effects are possible when using the strings in the scroll or peg box. The only printed example is found in Jon Deak's Surrealist Studies (1970).

4. The flicking of fingernails against a string (open, stopped, or dampened) produces a gentle but incisive percussion music.

5. Pizzicato Muta. This unusual pizzicato technique is adapted from the guitar and produces a sound similar to a pizzicato harmonic.[22]   The thumb is used as the generator while the lower part of the palm damps the string. I find myself still in the early laboratory stages with this technique and at this writing (December 1970) can only suggest that the first and second strings are useful. It is a question of experimentation and time until we know more of the potential of pizzicato muta.

---

[21] Recorded by Betram Turetzky for Medea Records: "The Virtuoso Double Bass" (1965).

[22] See the discussion on pizzicato harmonics in Chapter V.

Chapter II: New Directions in Bowing

Since the work of François Tourte (1747-1835) led to the "modern" bow, string players have been primarily involved in the following specific aspects of bowing techniques:

I. Sound

    A. Beauty [1]

    B. Power

    C. Control

II. Velocity

    A. On the string

    B. Off the string

Now, two-thirds through the twentieth century, we can clearly see the importance of coloration/registration, and the technique of bowing is developing beyond the concepts listed above into the following directions (the first two are traditional):

1. On and off

2. Up and down

3. Hair to wood (and vice versa)

4. Reverse bowing

5. Horizontal to diagonal (and vice versa)

ON AND OFF

The majority of arco techniques are done on the string; there is no need to concern ourselves with a review of these basic bowing matters. The "off the string" variety of bowing

---

[1] "Bel canto" as conceived by Auer, Casals, and other basically nineteenth-century artists, who developed twentieth-century string playing.

deals primarily with short, i.e., staccato, sounds, in which the bow is bounced/thrown "on and off" the string as in <u>spiccato</u> or <u>saltando.</u> These strokes sound like percussion and mix extremely well with left hand alone, <u>col legno,</u> and <u>ponticello pizzicato.</u> Percussive use of off-the-string bowing techniques includes jeté and richochet.

UP AND DOWN

This category includes the primary colors of bowing <u>sul tasto</u> (up), <u>normale</u> (middle), and <u>sul ponticello</u> (down), which have become more and more important. In fact, as this century's music has developed, one can clearly see the ascendance of tone color in the hierarchy of the components of music. We can understand this situation when we trace the interest in new sounds back to the post-Lisztian development of instrumental resources, with the newer "sound ideals" as a reaction against the nineteenth century distortion of "bel canto;" and note the late coming of age of certain instruments and the unwillingness of their pioneer practitioners to develop in the traditional (i. e., nineteenth century) manner.[2] Thus the people of this century are going beyond the notion of "sound as an end in itself" into new vistas. Bartolozzi's important work in woodwind multiphonics could not have been done if he had built his work on the ideals of the last century.

The development of these "new" sounds/colors ran parallel with the rise of completely serialized music, in which style more than primary color was needed to animate serialization. Therefore, the "up (<u>tasto</u>) and down (<u>ponticello</u>)" placement of the bow becomes a very important and vital part of twentieth-century bowing technique. The following example from <u>Concert Piece</u> (1962-1968) by Stephen Fisher gives the essential idea of the second category:

Example 1: <u>Concert Piece</u> (1962-1968), Stephen Fisher

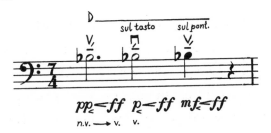

Note that each of the three B-flats has a different color. However, a differentiation between <u>sul tasto</u>, <u>normale</u>, and <u>sul ponticello</u> is possible to discern if the bow placement is possible to discern if the bow placement is correct. I mean that <u>ponticello</u> must mean

---

[2] A new world of sound is coming, exemplified by the work of musicians like the brilliant trombonist Stuart Dempster, clarinetist W. O. Smith, and the entire new work with percussion instruments.

almost on the bridge, a different notion than the older string players' concept of sul ponticello as four to five inches from the bridge. Look at the following illustration which depicts the proper bow placement:

Example 2:
    A. Sul tasto — on the fingerboard (not near the fingerboard)
    B. Sul ponticello — almost on the bridge (not merely near the bridge)

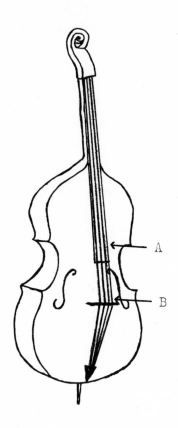

Thus the bow can move within a range of color possibilities: (1) down to normale, which
is approximately halfway between the end of the fingerboard (i. e., sul tasto); (2) up to
over the fingerboard (i. e., sul tasto); (3) down almost to the bridge (sul ponticello).
Before going on toward more complicated notions (registration, plus the idea of which part
of the bow to use, say punta or au talon, perhaps contrast between hair and wood), let us
go back to Example 1. When you add the "other" bowing directions, the dynamic instructions (note the complexity of serialized dynamics) and the vibrato instructions, the amal-
gam is a most complicated 7/4-measure at M. M. ♩ = 144!

Later in this composition, in measures (M.) 16-19, we find a series of 18 different notes,
of which 17 have timbral contrasts. Examination of Example 3 will show the bow placement
problems complicated by the six pizzicato notes.

Example 3: Concert Piece (1962-1968), Stephen Fisher

An idea of the potential in rapid-fire registration is clearly discerned in the following example. A performance at M. M. ♩ = 144, though virtuosic, is idiomatic and musically very striking.

Example 4: Concert Piece (1962-1968), Stephen Fisher

Shifts from sul tasto to sul ponticello are a feature of another chain of separate pitches with different coloration which comprises m. 147-156. Example 5 shows m. 147-149.

Example 5: Concert Piece (1962-1968), Stephen Fisher

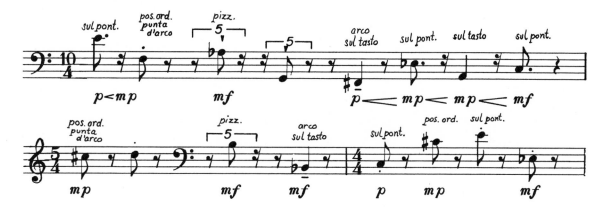

Before going on to the application of "up and down" while a note is being sustained, I should like to speculate about possibilities for these timbral changes. The addition of col legno tratto and battuto, left hand alone, and colorfully articulated pizzicato fill another lacuna in technique which will soon be idiomatic to the new contrabassist. See Example 6.

Example 6: <u>Systems</u> (1968), Richard Moryl

"UP AND DOWN" WHILE SUSTAINING A NOTE

A veritable Pandora's box was opened by John Cage in 1955 with his composition <u>26'</u> <u>I. 1499" for a String Player</u>, in which he inaugurated the idea of coloring a sustained note. Thus, a note will begin bowed <u>normale</u> and will change to <u>ponticello</u> (down) at its conclusion. For example, Cage calls for a <u>ponticello</u> to change to <u>normale</u>; then <u>normale</u> to <u>ponticello</u>; <u>tasto</u> to <u>normale</u>; <u>normale</u> to <u>tasto</u>; <u>tasto</u> to <u>ponticello</u>; and <u>ponticello</u> to <u>tasto</u>.

This concept is taken a step further in 1969 with ensemble use. The sound of four contrabasses coloring sustained notes is prominently heard in Donald Erb's <u>Basspiece</u> (1969), first movement, measures 6-8.

Example 7: <u>Basspiece</u> (1969), Donald Erb. Recorded by Bertram Turetsky on Desto Records

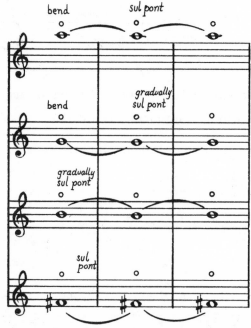

It is important, also, to note that Erb colors the chord microtonally as well. (See the indication "bend," meaning pulled-harmonics, in Chapter V.

The Cage notion of timbral shifting through changes of bow position became a most important component of Richard Moryl's <u>Systems</u> (1968). This unaccompanied piece is a very important sonority study, and the role of color is clearly described by the composer:

<u>Systems</u> explores the various string sonorities, and the possible ways of attacking each and every note. Combinations of the many string techniques, and multiple

changes of bow position during a tone, are employed.[3]

Here is the second phrase from <u>Systems</u>:

Example 8: <u>Systems</u> (1968), Richard Moryl

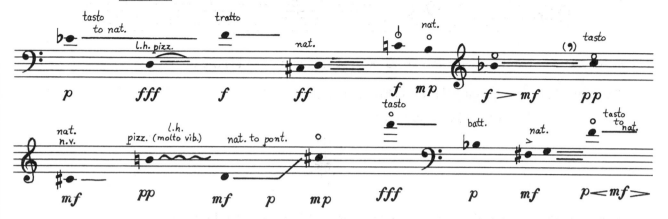

It begins with a timbral shift, with a left hand pizzicato, and then moves into a true
<u>Klangfarbenmelodie.</u>   An even more varied phrase is the final phrase on page 1, which adds
W. B. (with the back of the bow on the body of the instrument), right hand roll on wood, and
harmonics to the more standard pizzicato, <u>ponticello</u>, <u>secco</u>, <u>normale</u> (nat.), and <u>col legno</u>
<u>battuto</u>.

Example 9: <u>Systems</u> (1968), Richard Moryl

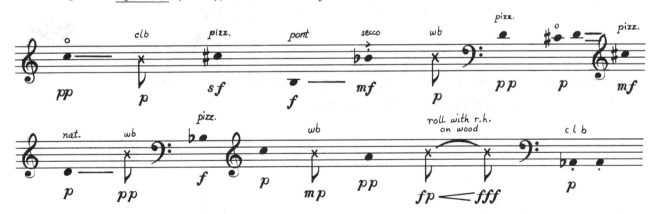

HAIR TO WOOD AND VICE VERSA

Another direction bowing is moving today is from hair (<u>normale</u>) to wood (<u>legno</u>).   The
twist of a wrist (r. h.) accomplishes this easily and quickly, producing a thorough change in
color.   The change can go to <u>col legno tratto</u>, <u>col legno battuto</u>, or one-half <u>legno</u>, with
all the resulting registrational/coloristic possibilities. These changes are possible in quite
rapidly shifting note-to-note sequences as well as in such sustained situations as —

---

[3] <u>Systems</u>, Richard Moryl.

Example 10: Hair to wood changes

The next few examples show where to bow, besides on the strings.

Example 11: Surrealist Studies (1970), Jon Deak

bow directly on bridge

Example 12: Capriccio per oboe a 11 archi (1964), K. Penderecki

arpeggio on four strings between bridge and tailpiece

play on tailpiece

play on bridge

Example 13: Threnody to the Victims of Hiroshima (1961), K. Penderecki

play between bridge and tailpiece

Example 14: <u>String Quartet II</u> (1963), Michael von Biel

    bow behind bridge, very close to bridge

    bow across tailpiece

    bow at middle of tailpiece

    (note that von Biel has no sign for bow across top of tailpiece)

    bow at base of tailpiece

    bow on side of bridge

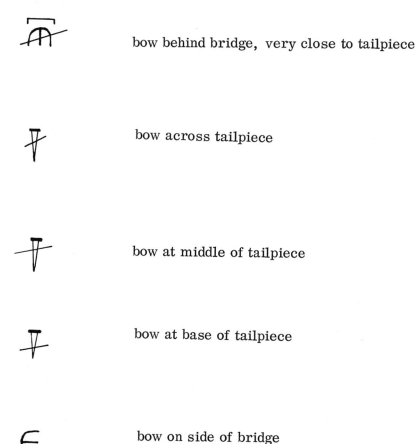

    bow behind bridge, very close to tailpiece

    bow across tailpiece

    bow at middle of tailpiece

    bow at base of tailpiece

    bow on side of bridge

Example 15: <u>Color Studies</u> (1969), Jon Deak

    bow vertically at side of bridge, producing groan

The registration possibilities of _legno_ are lightly touched on by Richard Moryl in _Systems_ (1968). The various tones sounded by changing the bow position are easily heard (see Chapter III).

Example 16: _Systems_, Richard Moryl

REVERSE BOWING

Using the bow upside down under the strings changes the arc of the strings and makes it possible to bow all the double stops on the G and E strings (the outside strings). Probably the earliest appearance in print is found in Peter Phillips' _Chimer_ (1963). In Phillips' _Sonata for String Bass_ (1964) the following use of reverse bow is found:

Example 17: _Sonata for String Bass_ (1964), Peter Phillips

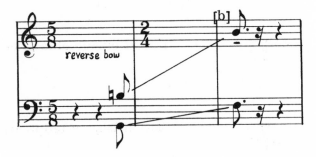

Barney Childs uses reverse bowing to play a complex harmonic double stop.

Example 18: _Mr. T, His Fancy_ (1967), Barney Childs

Thus we are now presented with these new possibilities: (a) harmonics on G and E, (b) stopped notes on G combined with harmonics on E, and (c) harmonics on B combined with stopped notes on E. Control is very difficult using reverse bowing. Composers should consult directly with a creative, concerned contrabassist and the latter should practice and experiment in this area as well.

BOWING "AF"

Jon Deak's <u>Color Studies for Contrabass</u> (1969) introduces in print the concept of bowed bi-tones (see Chapter I, p. 9).   The bassist is instructed to bow above the left hand fingers. Deak coined the designation "AF" ("above fingers") and notates the resultant pitches in cues directly above the standard ("place your finger here") notation.

Example 19: "Fog White," from <u>Color Studies for Contrabass</u> (1969), Jon Deak

The possibilities of AF are many, but the damage done by rosin getting all over the strings (in the lower positions) may eliminate its acceptance as a technique, even more than the reluctance of some performers to play <u>col legno</u>. [4]

The most well-known percussion technique in string writing is the use of <u>col legno</u> <u>battuto</u>. At this writing, the earliest usage known is found in the publication <u>Musical</u> <u>Humors</u> (1605) by Tobias Hume, who gave the following directions: "Drum this with the back of the bow." Thus this technique, despised by most string players because of presumed bow damage, is not an invention of the twentieth century but a technique that preceded the universal acceptance of the violin family!

Some of today's most brilliant sounding <u>col legno</u> writing is found in <u>Ricercar á 3</u> (1967) by Robert Erickson (who set this example against two tape-recorded tracks of fast pizzicato and various percussion sounds).

---

[4] It is amusing to note that Rogers in his <u>Art of Orchestration</u> speaks of a bassist refusing to play <u>col legno tratto tremolo</u>. This is not a universal situation today, and Rogers was clearly talking about one of his Eastman colleagues.

Example 20: Ricercar á 3 (1967), Robert Erickson

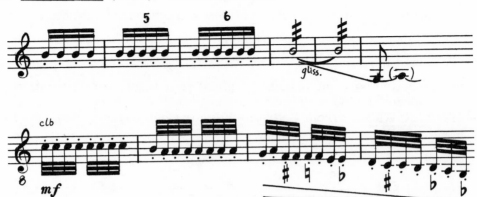

Donald Erb is very fond of the "quasi-marimba" sound of col legno battuto. His VII Miscellaneous (1964) for flute and contrabass makes an arresting use of this technique. Note the opening four measures which set the first movement into motion in a delightfully light manner.

Example 21: VII Miscellaneous (1964), Donald Erb. Recorded by the Turetskys on Medea Records.

He begins his Trio for Two (1968) with this bravura passage:

Example 22: Trio for Two (1968), Donald Erb. Recorded by the Turetskys on Ars Nova Records.

A few measures later (after employing vocal sounds with col legno tratto tremolo) an ascent to the top of the instrument's range is achieved in the following manner:

Example 23: Trio for Two (1968), Donald Erb

These fast-moving passages sound excellent, but the composer must remember that the technique required is not "stock in trade" for the contrabass player and that the bow is awkward, heavy, and long.

Col legno techniques can and must use registration as in traditionally bowed music. A lacuna must be utilized consciously is the "strike tone" produced by the wood of the bow hitting the string (which is open or stopped as the situation may call for). The frequency of the strike tone changes as the point of contact (i.e., the wood of the bow) changes up and down the length of the string. In fact, two pitches will be generated, the strike tone and the pitch of the length of the string. Higher frequencies are produced when the bow strikes near the bridge and lower frequencies as the bow moves toward the fingerboard. Experimentation in this area has produced and will produce very colorful and useful results for performers and composers.

In his quartet for one doublebass player, Inside (1969), Kenneth Gaburo makes use of a variety of col legno techniques. One is a colorful variety of col legno tratto in which the bow moves toward the bridge.

Example 24: Inside (1969), Kenneth Gaburo

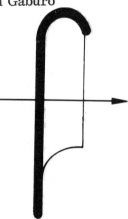

The opposite directions would also work. The notation is clear and for the retrograde the direction of the arrow could simply be changed. Gaburo also calls for a jeté col legno which is very attractive.

Example 25: Inside (1969), Kenneth Gaburo

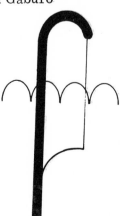

An interesting modification of col legno battuto is found in several scores of Maurico Kagel [5] and Kenneth Gaburo [6]. Gaburo calls for B. P. (bass bowed pizzicato — side of bow), which is technically col legno battuto plus arco spiccato and Kagel calls for one-half legno. These techniques are both the same, and the one-half legno seems to be a more clear designation. The sound is predominantly col legno battuto, but there is some of the "WSHHH" of the bow-hair mixed in. [7]

ANGLE OF BOW

Changing the "cutting" angle of the bow from the horizontal to a more diagonal position can produce groans and assorted random partials and sundry "noises." The colors change according to where you place the bow (tasto, normale, ponticello) as well as the angle and weight or pressure used.

Example 26: Color Studies for Contrabass (1969), Jon Deak

moving bow vertically, producing low belch or sigh intonation

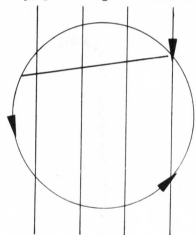

In the last few years the idea of circular bowing has been encountered. The next three examples will focus on circular bowing as explained and notated by three different composers.

---

[5] Sonant (1960) for harp, guitar, contrabass, and percussion.

[6] See Two (1963) for soprano, alto flute, and contrabass, and Antiphony IV (1966-1967) for piccolo, bass trombone, and contrabass.

[7] Bernard Rogers, in his Art of Orchestration, p. 20, mentions one-half legno: "When the bow is half-turned, so that both hair and wood engage the string, a rustling sound results." In researching this book, I learned why so many composers had told me that Rogers was one of the masters of orchestration.

Example 27: String Quartet II (1963), Michael von Biel
                    slow, repeated rotary motion of bow on string

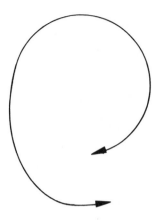

Example 28: Color Studies for Contrabass (1969), Jon Deak
                    elliptical motions

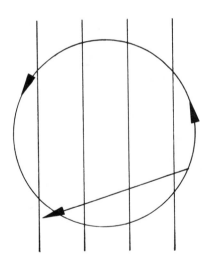

Example 29: <u>Logs</u> (1969), Paul Chihara.   Recorded by Bertram Turetsky
on CRI recordings.

> Circular bowing: Begin down-bow at the normal distance from the
> bridge and gradually slide over the fingerboard as the stroke
> approaches the tip.   Then return quickly and lightly <u>sul tasto</u>
> up-bow to the bridge.   No attempt need be made to make this
> stroke perfectly circular: rather a sighing sound, as con-
> tinuous and even as possible.

Chapter III: The Bass as a Drum: A Discussion of the Percussion
Parameter of Midcentury Writing for the Contrabass

The monumental transformation of the pianoforte by Cowell and Cage into a sound-producing instrument ranging from a gamelan to an eerie Celtic harp has had a parallel development in the percussive use of string instruments. Because of the great resonance of the contrabass, composers are beginning to use it percussively. The hands are the most practical sound generators, and we distinguish at least five different techniques — knuckle, palm, fingertip, fingernail, and cupped hand — which produce five very different timbres. These five can be employed to rap, tap, or slap the ribs, neck, top, back, bridge, scroll, tailpiece, or fingerboard. Combinations of these, as well as the numerous permutations available when using both hands, give composers and performers tremendous possibilities. However, players with pedigreed instruments are very discreet about tapping, rapping, and slapping, and the thought of using a bow or mallet to strike any part of the instrument except the scroll or the tailpiece is properly considered blasphemous.

Edward Diemente, whose Unvelopment (1968) for contrabass solo and wind ensemble makes extensive use of percussion techniques, explains in a letter to me his raison d'etrê and gives us a real insight into the motivation to use a string instrument in such a way:

> In Unvelopment, the places where I remember using percussive effects I thought at the time that there were musical ideas which could not be projected in the regular manner of traditional string technique. I found, for instance, that the Bass body was perfect for getting a very delicate 'bongo' effect by tapping the top of the instrument up near the shoulder and working down to the navel. No drum could get this unique sound.

Noteworthy use of the percussive potential is found in Mr. T., His Fancy (1967) by Barney Childs. [1]   The composer contrasts the sound of the fingers, thumbs, knuckle, and slap (i.e., four fingers) on the top and ribs of the instrument.   The movement also utilizes pizzicato (stopped notes, harmonics, behind the bridge), speech[2], and a pencil[3] used to generate three different types of sound.   Example 1 demonstrates Childs' solution to the notation problem and the employment of fingers, thumbs, knuckle, and slap.

The printing of the entire movement makes it possible to examine the techniques and their integration into the structure.   The use of the eraser and the body of the pencil[4] gives us a contrast not unlike that of normale contrasted with con sordino.   The "rattle"[5] sounds neo-electric, especially if the pencil is moved toward and away from the bridge, thus producing double strike tones.   A very perceptible crescendo in density is achieved in system 7 with the addition of speech and pizzicato beyond the bridge to the knuckle tap.   Many permutations come to mind while observing and playing this phrase, and perhaps this mixing of techniques might be most important and meaningful to composers in the future.

In Conversations for Solo Contrabass (1968), Charles Whittenberg makes a sparse use of percussion effects and achieves a very tight integration.[6]   Note the initial appearance in which a finger roll crescendoes into the F♯-C♯ (played by the left hand alone) which proceeds to the sustained E^2.

---

[1] Recorded by the author for Ars Nova records.

[2] See chapter IV.

[3] A dowel is employed by Robert Erickson in Ricercar á 3 (1967).

[4] Performers should note that if the pencil is invisible to the audience prior to the "rattle" the effect is heightened considerably.

[5] See system 3, Example 1.   Erickson makes use of this effect prior to Childs, but the latter is responsible for the name.

[6] Thrones (1966) by Richard Swift also has an outstanding integration of percussion writing with much "behind the bridge" writing.

Example 1: <u>Mr. T., His Fancy</u>, Barney Childs

Movement II

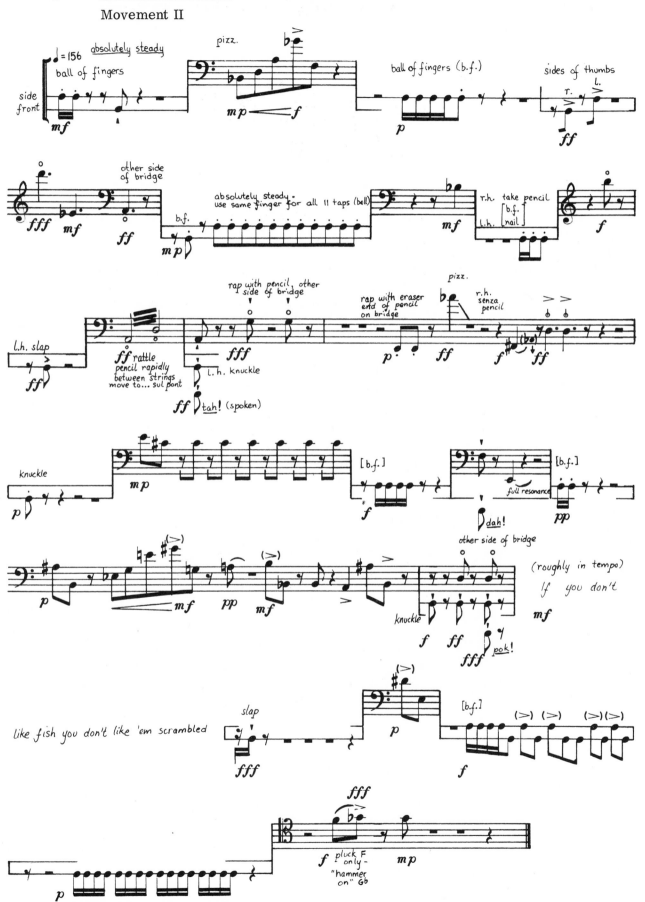

Example 2: Conversations for Solo Contrabass (1968), Charles Whittenberg.

Whittenberg differentiates between fingers and palm and carefully proposes the idea of pitch outline in his preface, where he presents a notation:

> Clefs and position of noteheads indicate where to strike the body of the instrument. The total body from just above the end-piece to the range of wood opposite the fingerboard is used in this work. Middle C is indicated midway between the fingerboard and the lowest part of the instrument.

Balances (1963) by Ramon Sender (amplified violin, viola, cello, and contrabass) is a pioneering work in percussion writing for string instruments. Sender makes elegant use of the percussion parameter, which he presents in a fanciful notation.

Example 3: Balances (1963), Ramon Sender

        finger taps

        fingernail taps

        tailpiece tapped with fingernail

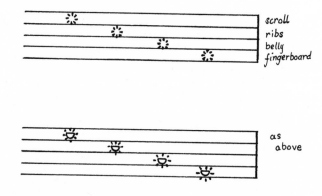

In his <u>Bass: A Theater Piece in Open Style for String Bass, Player, Tape and Film</u> (1966), Larry Austin makes extensive and perhaps violent use of percussion writing. He is interested in timbre rather than approximate pitch and has devised a very clear notation to articulate his ideas:

Fb	= fingerboard
W	= wood of bow
Fst	= fist
B	= back of bass
F	= front of bass
Bw	= bow
p	= palm of hand

<u>Exit Music for 12 Players</u> (1968) by George Burt includes percussion effects for strings in three categories: high, low, and metal tapping. These sounds are notated in the following way:

T/b	=	tap tail of instrument with bow
T/f	=	tap with fingers on lower front of the instrument
T/bonMS	=	tap either music stand or chair legs (metal pair) with bow.
		Rhythms are indicated with an X.

Another interesting notation is found in <u>Phantasmagoria</u> (1968) by Wayne Peterson, who articulates his colorful contrabass percussion music in a most clear and specific notation that stems from traditional percussion notation. The contrabass part is written on two separate staves with the staff for percussion being divided into three parts:

    side_____

    belly_____

    tailpiece_____

Thus the specifically designated sound generators (i. e., knuckle, left hand slap, etc.) are clearly notated in rhythm. Peterson uses an inverted Bartok pizzicato ( ) to indicate the thumb and arabic numerals for the other fingers. This notation is most exact and is very clear for the performer.

Meyer Kupferman, in his <u>Infinities 24</u> (1968) for contrabass and tape, differentiates between the sound of fingers and knuckles and calls for the use of a hard timpani stick (r. h.) on the strings with random pitches on the fingerboard (l. h.)

Example 4: <u>Infinities</u> 24 (1968), Meyer Kupferman

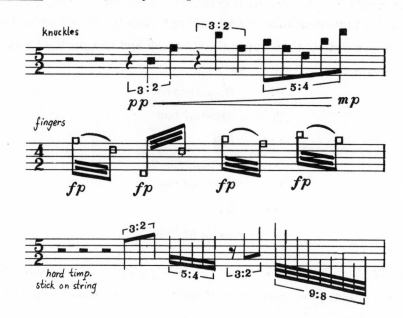

Note from the above example that the composer calls for various timbres, thus differing from some of the composers who are mostly interested in rhythmic aspects.

The percussion subphrase from <u>Logs</u> (1969) by Paul Chihara is a significant example of imaginative contrasting of various percussive timbres in a very brief time span.

Example 5: <u>Logs</u> (1969), Paul Chihara

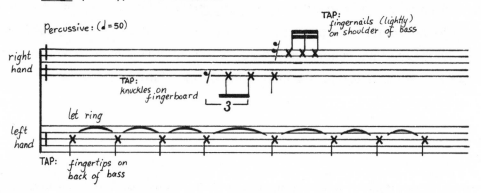

The possibilities for using percussion instruments in conjunction with the contrabass are tremendous (for example: maracas, hi-hat cymbals, and triangles). Alvin Curran in <u>Homemade</u> (1968) calls for these and other exotica. My dear friend, teacher, and favorite contrabassist, David Walter, describes in a letter to me an incredible job he played with a Rhumba Band in 1934-1935:

> I Pizzed on 1, 4, 7; slapped (open-palm) the strings against the fingerboard
> on 2, 3, 6, 8; struck a hi-hat cymbal on 3 and 7; held a maraca in my right
> hand for 8-beat rattle; and kept a paper between fingerboard and strings with
> my left hand to get a "jawbone" rattle.

On top of this he also threw in some "self-conscious shouts of <u>'agua, agua,</u>' 'caliente,' ' arriba, ' and 'ole.'' This amusing description of what some Latin and commercial bassists were doing 30 years ago certainly foreshadows the avant-garde use of "extra-contrabass-generated" sounds and the doubling or tripling called for by such composers as Alvin Curran and David Reck.

Thomas Frederickson, in his Music for Five Instruments (1965), conjures up a magical musical moment (second only to Karl Ditters von Dittersdorf's "inspired" use of the viola playing bass to the contrabass in his Symphonia concertante) when a xylophone cadenza is accompanied by a contrabass "percussion" part. He differentiates between thumb, cupped hand, fingernails, and knuckles as sound generators as well as specifying the areas of the instrument to slap, rap, and tap. This is the most extensive and demanding percussion part in the literature known to me.

Example 6: Music for Five Instruments (1965), Thomas Frederickson

Kenneth Gaburo makes extensive use of the percussion parameter in his colorful and virtuosic <u>Inside</u> (1969).   He has devised an excellent notation system:

a = knuckle on bass shoulder (l.h.)

b = palm of hand on bass shoulder (l.h.)

c = fingertips on bass shoulder (l.h.)

d = fingernail clicks on bass shoulder (l.h.)

e = cupped hand on bass shoulder (l.h.)

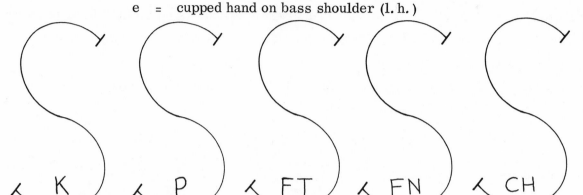

The remainder of these techniques use the bow and were therefore discussed in Chapter II.

The similarity between contrabass fingertapping and woodwind key clicking is explored by Sydney Hodkinson in his <u>Interplay</u> (1966) for flute (alto flute and piccolo), Bb clarinet (saxophone and Eb clarinet), percussion and contrabass.   An example is found at rehearsal letter H in Example 7.

Example 7: <u>Interplay</u> (1966), Sydney Hodkinson

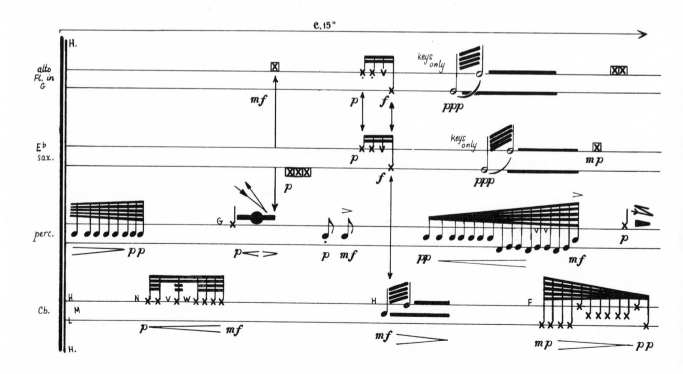

Note that the composer is concerned primarily with sound and timbre and leaves the choice of the "striking area" to the performer.

Frederickson's Music for Doublebass Alone (1963) makes the first significant use of this technique. His coupling of melodic fragments (played left hand alone) over a drone (played pizzicato tremolo) telescoped the extended two part writing found in the Ricercar á 3 (1967) by Robert Erickson. To this date the accompaniment, so to speak, for left hand alone has consisted of pizzicato drones. Suggestions: arco tremolo (tasto, normale, or ponticello); knuckles on any part of the instrument; fingertips on any part of the instrument; fingernails on any part of the instrument. Speculation about future development of this technique will probably be in the realm of contrasting pizzicato with col legno battuto, and left hand alone.

So far in this study, the performer's hands on the instrument have been the prime sound generators. Peter Phillips, in his Divertimento for Three String Basses (1968) makes use of the hands alone as generators as well as the sound source. This is achieved by using handclapping, finger snapping, and instrumental tapping to produce a fascinating audiovisual collage of percussion sights and sounds.

Example 8: Divertimento for Three String Basses (1968), Peter Phillips

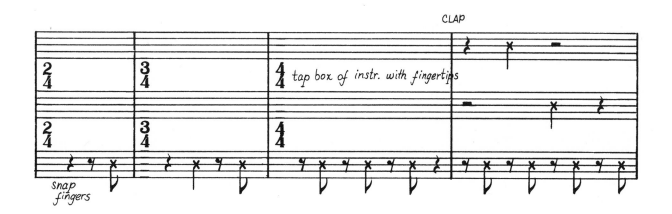

Eugene Kurtz makes extensive use of percussion writing in his Improvisation for Contrabass (1968). Utilized are col legno battuto, fingertips and knuckle rapping, finger snapping, and some powerful slapping effects.

Example 9: <u>Improvisation for Contrabass</u> (1968), Eugene Kurtz

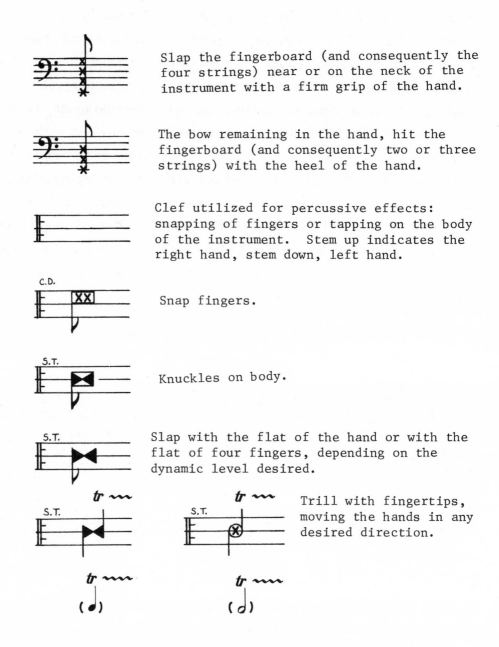

Slap the fingerboard (and consequently the four strings) near or on the neck of the instrument with a firm grip of the hand.

The bow remaining in the hand, hit the fingerboard (and consequently two or three strings) with the heel of the hand.

Clef utilized for percussive effects: snapping of fingers or tapping on the body of the instrument. Stem up indicates the right hand, stem down, left hand.

Snap fingers.

Knuckles on body.

Slap with the flat of the hand or with the flat of four fingers, depending on the dynamic level desired.

Trill with fingertips, moving the hands in any desired direction.

In his 1969 <u>Duo for Trumpet and Doublebass</u>, William Sydeman uses an amplifier which insures projection of all available nuances of his percussion writing for the contrabass. Sydeman gives a chart indicating where the sounds are to be produced:

Example 10: <u>Duo for Trumpet and Doublebass</u> (1969), William Sydeman

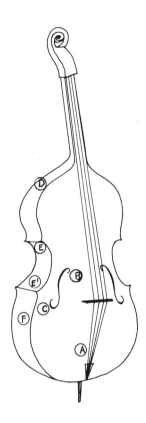

Three new techniques are found in the fourth and fifth movements: (1) there is bounce bow, <u>F</u> as jeté from top to bottom of curve (at E) to tremolo; (2) a fascinating texture (reminiscent of movements in Donald Erb's <u>In No Strange Land</u> [1968]) is manufactured by tapping <u>BC</u> with fingers while the trumpet "hits palm against mouthpiece"; and (3) Sydeman gives directions for a neo-electronic ostinato in movement four: "<u>Left hand</u>: with a large wooden salad tossing spoon strikes strings on far side of bridge. Let spoon bounce freely... randomly striking different strings to create a chaotic cacophonic racket. <u>Right hand</u>: occasionally tap side of fingerboard." During (3), the amplifier should be at the highest level short of feedback.

Jogi Yuasa in <u>Triplicity for Contrabass</u> (1970) makes colorful use of percussion techniques. He calls for fingertip; fingernail; knuckle-and palm-generated sounds to be produced on the

back of the instrument = B,

shoulder of the instrument = S,

front of the instrument = F, and

upper edge of the waist of the instrument = W.

A vibe mallet is used to strike the tailpiece and play on the strings behind the bridge. These two very different sound sources are contrasted throughout the composition. A most colorful modification of col legno battuto is also employed — the substitution of a maraca for the bow.

Lou Harrison sums up my feelings about treating the contrabass as a percussion instrument. In his "Introductory Notes" to the Suite for Symphonic Strings (1960-1963) he writes: "I think that any sound that can be generated by a musical instrument is legitimate, so long as that method does not injure the instrument." In the first movement, "Estampie," Mr. Harrison writes for contrabass divisi a 2, making use of the fingers on one part and col legno below the bridge on the other.

Example 11: Suite for Symphonic Strings (1960-1963), Lou Harrison

To insure that the proper sounds are produced the composer adds the following picture and words about the finger-drumming in the "Introductory Notes":

We found that with two or three fingers beaten, the contrabass emits a sonorous 'drumming' . . . the striking of the strings of the contra-bass col legno below the bridge will produce a slightly 'ping' semi-pitched drumming, whose sound will suggest both that of the marimbula and that of certain Oriental drums.

In the penultimate movement, "Rondo," Harrison introduces something he calls the "thwack," produced by striking the top of the middle of the bridge col legno. Donald Erb, in the first movement of Reconnaissance (1967) calls for something similar in sound and less dangerous to the instrument.

Example 12: Reconnaissance (1967), Donald Erb

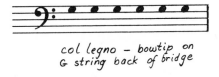

col legno - bowtip on
G string back of bridge

Example 13: Suite for Symphonic Strings (1960-1963), Lou Harrison

on the body

Cb.

Thus we see Harrison using all three of his percussion techniques in the Rondo of his Suite. To add some contrast, he also alternates between solo and tutti. In his informative and disarming introduction we are told that "the general effect of these devices will suggest (beyond their rhythmic impact) the extraneous sounds made by some instruments (here on a large scale) as well as the bumps and thuds made by imaginary dancers dancing to the music."[7]

RUB SOUNDS

Rub sounds are another adoption of new percussion techniques and are related to the timbre of woodwind and brass air sounds. This category is a lacuna with very few printed examples.

My presentation here will follow where to rub, and what to rub with. The body of the bass is the most proper and obvious place to begin. We use the area from the bridge to the shoulders with greatest physical or geographical ease. Circular motions of the flat hand or palm, slow or fast, give a continuous "whooshy" sound whereas short vertical movements will supply the accents and discontinuous activities. Crescendi and diminuendi are possible but it is important to note that the basic dynamic level is low (i.e., p-mp). These sounds mix very well, but don't expect to hear them readily as one level of a complex multilayered texture. An amplified bass would be able to solve this and in the very near future amplified rub sounds might very well become as much a cliché as ponticello did in the 1950's.

The "tambourine roll" used by percussionists to make tympani and bass drum heads "screech" is also an excellent addition to the always growing rub-sound palette. A part of the table (top) of the bass where rosin might collect is the best place for this, since the relaxed finger will find some cohesion to produce this sound. This sound (a friction rub) is not an "all weather" technique, unless the instrument is coated with rosin and/or dust, or the finger has some natural adhesive agents.

The strings are the other principal area for rub sounds and the generators include wood, flesh, metal, fingernail, and cloth. Thus col legno tratto could be considered an old and well-known part of this technique. It should be noted that this technique has not gained popularity among string players, and that also one should "rosin" the stick of the bow if he

---

[7] Suite for Symphonic Strings (1960-1963), Lou Harrison.

really wants <u>tratto</u> to sound above ppp. "Whooshy" aereated sounds can be produced by a gentle rubbing of one's fingers or palms on the strings. Random harmonics are produced and the sound has been likened to the wind-activated Aeolian harp.

Rubbing of wood, coins, and other metal objects on the strings produces a rasp (or scratch) tinged with the overtones of the string being attacked. Larry Austin has made effective use of this technique in <u>Bass</u> (1966).

Rubbing of the string with the fingernail produces a muted, more refined version of the above. Frank McCarty used the fingernail rub in <u>Bert Bells, Bows, Balls the Bass</u> (1970) I used it as one layer of a four-track mix on the opening of the CRI recording of Paul Chihara's <u>Logs</u> (1969). The mix is on an open E and consists of one track doing the circular bowing (see Chapter II, page 28; the second track is pizzicato tremolo; the third has the fingernail rub; and the fourth has drumming with the thumb and third finger (r. h.) on the opening string. (Listen to this colorful texture on the enclosed LP.)

In conclusion, the sound of a cloth (chamois or regular rag) rubbing like a string player does to clean off the rosin has some of the "gutsier" sound in the realm of rub sounds.

1. A very subtle and soft drumming is produced by oscillating the thumb and the second or third finger on the string. The differentiation of <u>tasto</u>, <u>normale</u>, and <u>ponticello</u> does not exist but this is such a distinctive color that it doesn't seem to need any assistance.

2. Another effective drumming can be produced by the use of thimbles on the fingers. Metal and plastic thimbles sound different and a mix is possible.

3. Fingering the string while another performer rolls on it with mallets and the use of superball mallets on the strings hold great potential for contrabass percussion composition. The noted percussionist John Bergamo said to me, in the winder of 1970, that "We're bowing cymbals, vibes, and gongs, and you're slapping, rapping, and tapping your instrument." For those who have been wondering where this percussion madness may lead, I must say that Robert Erickson succeeded in making this noble instrument sound like a sitar, and I hear an incredible percussion ensemble inside my instrument. I'm hoping some composers will let it out.

4. To conclude this chapter it might be fitting to present a "new timbral development from the Baroque." Heinrich Biber (1644-1704) in his <u>Battalia for Strings and Continuo</u> wrote a "March," in which the violin has to imitate a fife, and the double bass a drum. Biber wrote: "Where the drum is heard in the bass, a piece of paper must be used on the string...." This effect was not "bel canto"; timbral experimentation has always been a concern of composers and performers from the very wellsprings of music.

Chapter IV: Vocal and Speech Sounds

A Parameter of Instrumental Technique

The concept of using vocal sounds as a parameter of instrumental technique has become more and more significant and widespread since the early 1960's. The use of these techniques was inevitable because of:

1. The composer's quest for new sounds,

2. the new relation between composer and performer, and

3. the new performer's involvement with the timbral potential of his instrument. [1]

A most precise and illuminating statement discussing the raison d'être of using these techniques was articulated by Donald Erb, who wrote to me:

> Music is made by a performer. It comes from him rather than from his instrument, the instrument being merely a vehicle. Therefore it seems logical that any sound a performer can make may be used in a musical composition.

And there are the many timbral changes and extensions of possible attacks of woodwind and brass players, as well as the potential of vocal sounds used orchestrally, rhythmically, and in the numerous ways presented in this chapter.

Back in the 1940's, Benny Goodman featured an innovative jazz contrabassist who made famous the first technique I will discuss, a simple and obvious use of vocal sounds as a contrabass technique: the singing or humming in octaves with the instrument (arco or pizzicato). Leroy "Slam" Stewart made this technique internationally known three decades ago. An excellent example of this technique is found in Barney Childs' Jack's New Bag. [2]

---

[1] Bertram Turetzky, "Notes on the Bass," Source (Jan. 1967), 1:1.

[2] An earlier example is the 1961 Trio for valve trombone, contrabass and percussion of Kim Richmond. The last movement of Childs' Mr. T., His Fancy (1967) also has a memorable use of the sing along technique. It is recorded by the author on Ars Nova records.

Example 1: Jack's New Bag (1966), Barney Childs

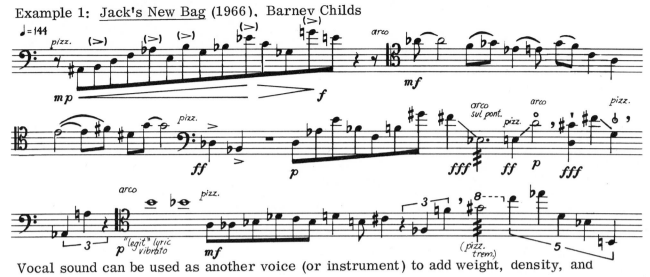

Vocal sound can be used as another voice (or instrument) to add weight, density, and another sound to those played by the contrabass.

Example 2: Automobile (1965), Russell Peck

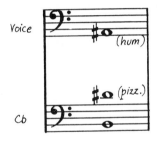

Example 3: One db (1968), Russell Peck

Left hand pizzicato can be added to textures like the above to "thicken the plot."

Example 4: Trio for Two (1968), Donald Erb[3]

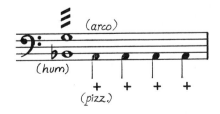

---

[3] Recorded by the author and Mrs. Turetzky on Ars Nova records.

Jacob Druckman in <u>Valentine</u> (1969) for solo contrabass makes use of vocal and speech sound not only mixed with instrumental sound but also coming out of instrumental sound.

Example 5: <u>Valentine</u> (1969), Jacob Druckman

This example is of the latter technique, obviously, and if the G♯s started and ended together the mixture of vocal and instrumental timbre would be the result. These techniques shod much potential for investigation in the coming years.

Speech sounds can accent, color, or articulate instrumental sounds in a most marked and/or theatrical manner.

Example 6: <u>Conversations</u> (1968), Charles Whittenberg

Example 7: <u>Ricercar á 3</u> (1967), Robert Erickson[4]

The next employment of the performer's vocal resources is rare and may never become common practice. The pioneer and most extravagant use of this technique is found in Russell Peck's <u>Automobile</u> (1965). This example might simply be referred to as "add-a-line."

---

[4] Recorded by the author on Ars Nova Records

Example 8: <u>Automobile</u> (1965), Russell Peck

While studying Peck's chamber music, I was struck by the frequency of his use of vocal

sounds. When I questioned him, he responded with the following statement:

> Some years ago I worked out a great number of possibilities of
> combined vocal and instrumental sounds for the trombone for
> use in Cacioppo's <u>Advance of the Fungii.</u> I became very in-
> terested in the resonances produced by vocal sound near the
> sounding body of an instrument (like the contrabass) or where
> the vocal source is part of the sounding body — as in the case
> of wind instruments. The proximity of the voice and instru-
> ment can produce either profuse beat patterns or provide
> subtle reinforcements of harmonics inherent in the instrument.

Donald Erb uses this two-part writing technique in a most colorful way and produces a

"hair raising" textural effect in this passage, set in contrary motion, from his <u>Trio for</u>

<u>Two</u> (1968).

Example 9: <u>Trio for Two</u> (1968), Donald Erb

Maurico Kagel also uses two-parts, but in a random manner; in his "Faites Otre Jeu II" of <u>Sonant</u> (1960) he writes: "Pizzicatolike sounds, made with a closed mouth, are to be added ad libitum. The pitch and intensity should be almost that of the instrumental sound."

In <u>Pajazzo</u> (1963) for eight jazz musicians, conductor, and audience, Folke Rabe makes colorful use of two-part writing. The following are examples:

> <u>Pizz</u>   PLAY SOUNDS AND IMITATE SIMULTANEOUSLY WITH YOUR
> <u>Arco</u>   VOICE

and

> MUMBLE AND HUM WHILE ACTIVELY PLAYING

and then, to heighten the overall sound and theatrical picture, Rabe adds the following:

> SING INTO YOUR OR OTHER MUSICIAN'S INSTRUMENT!

The use of words vocalized by the performer constitutes an extension of two-part writing, providing a more contrasted sound source than the wordless humming of the previous example.[5] The primary source, at this writing, is Elliot Schwartz's <u>Dialogue for Solo Contrabass</u> (1966).

Example 10: <u>Dialogue for Solo Contrabass</u> (1966), Elliot Schwartz

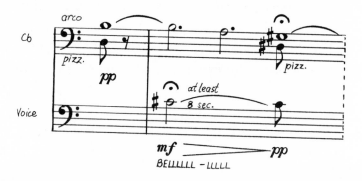

---

[5] Most bassists, while humming, would have a natural tendency to try to imitate the sound of their instruments, and words would be a distinctive second voice.

I found a most arresting use of humming and singing (in canon and echo) by instrumentalists already referred to in the Lorca settings of George Crumb:

Example 11: <u>Songs, Drones, and Refrains of Death</u> (1969), George Crumb

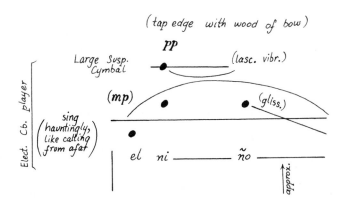

Talking has been used by several composers with excellent results. In <u>Pajazzo</u> (1963)
by Folke Rabe, performers receive the following instructions:

> Play actively and count aloud using the following numbers
> irreg. ; gradually stop playing: 9826 3 8 76 041 65
> 4 9294 6 593 05 4 371 83

In the "Pièce de Résistance" movement of <u>Sonant</u>, Kagel calls for speaking and whispering
ad libitum. The players are told to talk throughout the movement ("Fin II," "Invitation au
Jeu," and "Voix"). It is interesting to note that its conversation is measured in seconds
and the dynamics are given; also a choice of German, French, or English is offered.

Pauline Oliveros makes use of the lecture[6] in her <u>Doublebasses at Twenty Paces</u> (1968)
when she requests her performers to tell the audience what type of bow they use (and why)
and to discuss the "nationality" of their instruments. These lectures contribute a great
deal to the shape of the work as well as the general mood of this theater piece.

Ensemble speaking can also be used to color instrumental sounds:

---

[6] The first lecture piece known to me is Robert Ashley's <u>Trio III</u> (1963). It was not
included in the body of this article because the instrument that one should lecture about is
not specified in the score.

Example 12: <u>Songs, Drones, and Refrains of Death</u> (1969), George Crumb

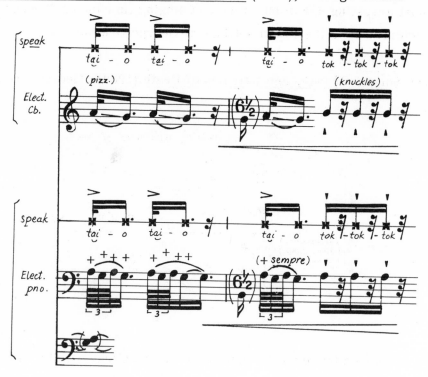

A highly structured use of speech sound is the canon, as found in works by David Cope and David Reck.[7] In <u>Cycles</u> (1969), for flute and contrabass, Cope makes use of a speech canon in echo. The text is given to the flutist, with a mf dynamic, while the contrabass directions are "speak softly, follow after first voice — "echo," which insures the results.

The Schwartz <u>Dialogue</u> has a fine example of speaking combined with instrumental sound.

Example 13: <u>Dialogue</u> (1966), Elliot Schwartz

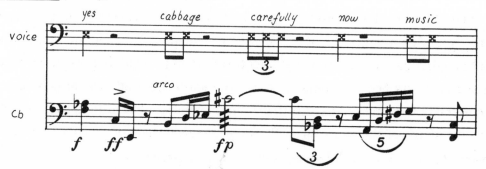

Some of the most colorful and integrated uses of the vocal parameters are found in the <u>Surrealist Studies</u> (1970) by Jon Deak. The mixture of pitched and unpitched (and/or unvoiced) materials is most imaginative and adds a dimension hitherto unknown.

---

[7] <u>Night Sounds (and Dream</u>) (1965), David Reck.

Example 14: "The Two Sisters" (Giorgio Dechirico), from

Surrealist Studies (1970), Jon Deak

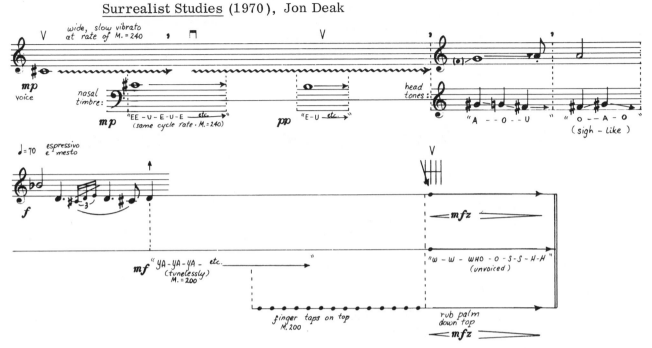

Shouts or vocal exclamations work very well and can painlessly coerce the audiences into more intense and concentrated listening. An integrated example is from Spectra (1966) by Richard Felciano. [8]

Example 15: Spectra (1966), Richard Felciano

Most expressive dramatic use of the ensemble shout is found in George Crumb's Songs, Drones, and Refrains of Death. This example is from a setting of Garcia Lorca's La Guitarra.

---

[8] Recorded by the author and Mrs. Turetzky on Ars Nova records.

Example 16: <u>Songs, Drones, and Refrains of Death</u> (1969), George Crumb

Let us now discuss the use of whispering, a very colorful and theatrical technique. Note the dramatic use of the contrabass being set in hocket with the soprano part. [9]

Example 17: Three Madrigals, for Soprano, Vibraphone and Contrabass (1965),
George Crumb

Next is an example of whispering used in an almost atmospheric context in the highly innovative Dialogue by Elliot Schwartz.

Example 18: Dialogue for Solo Contrabass (1966), Elliot Schwartz

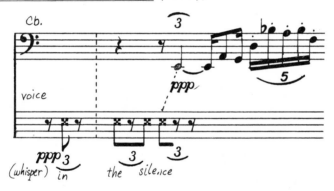

The combination of singing, whispering, and instrumental sounds is found in this work.

Example 19: Dialogue for Solo Contrabass (1966), Elliot Schwartz

The whisper mixes well with sung, spoken, or instrumental sound. A good example of such a "mix" is found in the last of David Reck's Night Sounds (and Dream) (1965).

---

[9] The contrabassist also plays a C (an octave below middle C) pizzicato tremolo throughout.

Example 20: <u>Night Sounds (and Dream)</u> (1965), David Reck

Numerous examples of ensemble whispering used in "mix" with instrument shouts (in the same manner as the ensemble shouts were used) are found in this previously mentioned work of George Crumb.

Example 21: <u>Songs, Drones, and Refrains of Death</u> (1969), George Crumb

The tongue click [10] (or cluck) was introduced into the contrabass literature in 1968 by Donald Erb. In the first example from Trio for Two he uses the clicking to lead into a left-hand-alone passage:

Example 22: Trio for Two (1968), Donald Erb

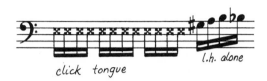

The second use of the tongue click is integrated with a pizzicato section, providing two separate parts:

Example 23: Trio for Two (1968), Donald Erb

The following modifications of this technique are used by Kenneth Gaburo in Inside (1969):

M = finger snap and mouth click
X

M_____ 0 = finger snap and mouth click (together), followed by whistle.
X

M is very similar to a knuckle rap on the shoulder of the instrument; this similarity of these
X
three sounds is demonstrated in the taped examples. The latter multiphonic sounds very well and constitutes a significant contribution.

Tongue clicks (high and low) are employed by George Crumb. The example chosen has the clicks set in hocket with guitar (while percussion II plays on open strings with hard mallets).

---

[10] Velar click, produced by pulling the tongue from the upper inside gum, not a retroflex click.

Example 24: <u>Songs, Drones, and Refrains of Death</u> (1969), George Crumb

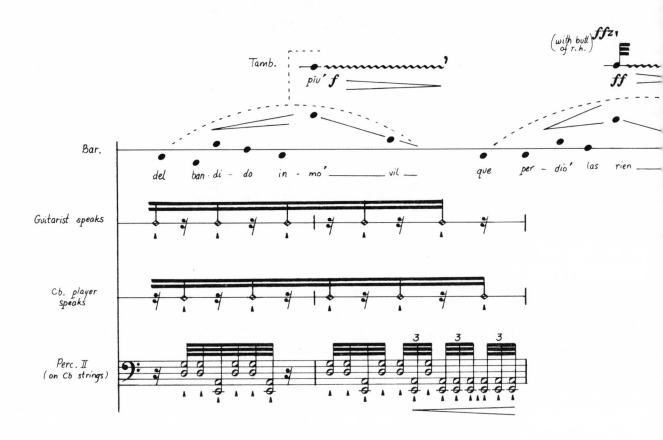

The low-pitched tongue click is very similar in sound to a knuckle rap on the shoulder of the bass.   Contrasts and/or mixes are available and very effective.   Any pitched tongue click provides a colorful mix with a pizzicato and a good blend with <u>col legno battuto</u> notes. These ideas are virgin territory and are in need of exploration.

Crumb is also the first composer to mix percussive play on the contrabass with vocal sounds — a memorable mixture of new timbral resources! In fact, this score is the best source book of exquisite usage of ensemble vocal and speech sounds known to me.

Example 25: <u>Songs, Drones, and Refrains of Death</u> (1969), George Crumb

In researching this paper, I found no example of speech (i. e., talking), vocalizing, humming, whispering, exclamation, whistling, etc., used in a contrapuntal manner. Experimentation with the possibilities of composing three, four, or five parts for one performer would be sonically spectacular, despite the complexity and versatility demanded. This area is clearly a lacuna waiting for future investigation.

The most significant large-scale use of these techniques in a solo work is found in Kenneth Gaburo's <u>Inside — A Quartet for One Doublebass Player</u> (1969) using

1. voiced phonemes derived from the word "inside,"
2. "extra-vocal" sounds, e.g., kissing, rolled <u>r</u>,
3. bass effects which employ the use of the strings, and
4. bass effects which do not employ the use of the strings.

This work is an invaluable sourcebook for integration of vocal and instrumental sounds.

An in-depth discussion of ensemble speech and/or vocal techniques is out of the range of this paper, but these possibilities are explored imaginatively in <u>Interplay</u> (1966) by Sydney Hodkinson and in <u>Limelight</u> (1968) by Klaus von Wrochem, and I will discuss these two pieces from this viewpoint.

Klaus von Wrochem makes use of ensemble vocal and speech sounds in several varied ways. First is a section in which he asks the performer to "play his instrument(s) and shout (voice) with the greatest possible independence, loudness, cruelty." Later, he calls for the performers (flute, violin, two contrabasses, and percussion) to sing specified pitches as they play other notes. The following example depicts the resulting pitch complex with the black notes being sung (without vibrato) and the others being instrumental.

Example 26: <u>Limelight</u> (1968), Klaus von Wrochem

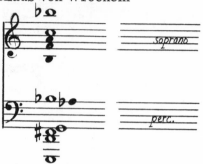

Vibrato is added and then parts, in glissandi, move toward a very excited section where the performers are asked to talk or read from Joyce, Beckett, or a newspaper in between instrumental events of dynamic and bravura character. The piece ends with the ensemble vocalizing while playing, thus producing a stunning texture which combines whistling, vocalizing, and instrumental sound.

Example 27: <u>Limelight</u> (1968), Klaus von Wrochem

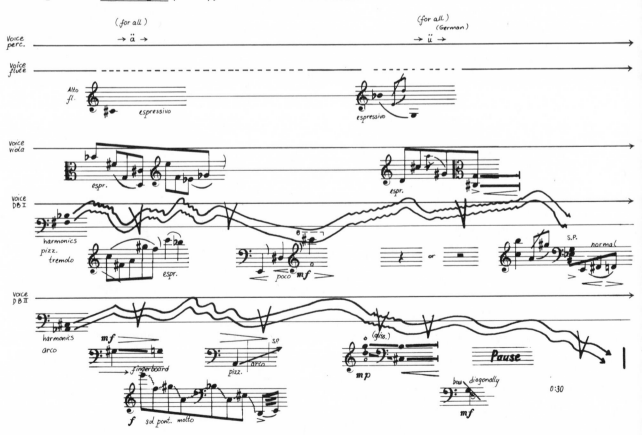

Sydney Hodkinson combines speech and vocal sounds (notated: high, middle, low) spoken (or blown) through a flute with normally-produced vocal sounds and places them against various percussion effects. Although brief, this section is a fine example of elegantly integrated ensemble vocal and speech writing.

Example 28: <u>Interplay</u> (1966), Sydney Hodkinson

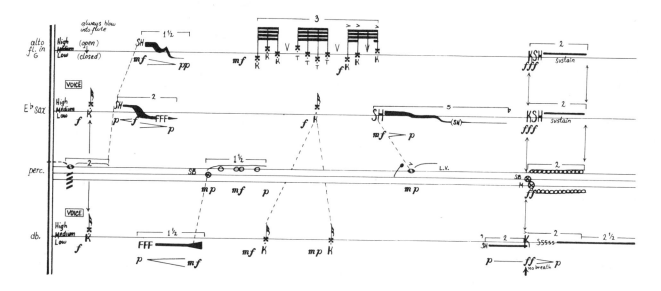

As this chapter closes, it should be clear to the reader that the material presented is but an introduction to a vast uncharted area. I have endeavored to show various usages of vocal and speech techniques without setting critical evaluations above categorization and notational codification. It is too early to worry about this. It is time to inspire composers to work in this area; to discover the resources of individual performers; to build a new literature and performance tradition. Then we will return to those more scholarly problems.

Chapter V: Harmonics

Harmonics are the traditional and obvious route out of the standard frequency spectrum of the contrabass. Once considered virtuoso material, harmonics were usually studied just prior to the solo repertoire of the concert artist. Today, because of their frequent use in twentieth century music, their place in the training sequence is beginning to change.

The contrabassist used natural harmonics almost exclusively until the beginning of the twentieth century. We first encounter them in concerti about 1750. [1] The composers used harmonics in two ways, best shown in the Dittersdorf Concerto in Eb Major. First, brief arpeggiated figures in the violin or viola range (Example 1).

Example 1: Concerto in Eb Major, Dittersdorf [2]

Second, hornlike fanfare motifs in a playful canonic dialogue with the strings (Example 2).

Example 2: Concerto in Eb Major, Dittersdorf

---

[1] The first extensive use of natural harmonics in violin music occurs in Mondonville's Les sons harmoniques, Op. 4 (1738) and the first exposition of artificial and natural harmonics is found in a Minuet by L'Abbe le Fils in 1761.

[2] The solo part is played in D major with a scordatura Ab, Eb, Bb, F.

After the early classical composers we find a more extended range and use of harmonics. On the first string, partials up to the third octave are often used. On the second string, partials up to the flat seventh, and on the lower strings up to the second fifth, are used. The following passage from the "Dragonetti" [3] Concerto is a fine example of this more advanced writing:

Example 3: "Dragonetti" Concerto

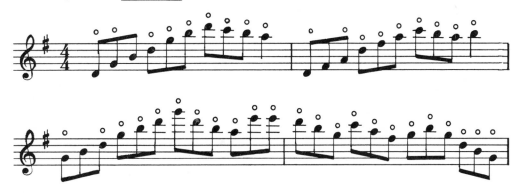

Giovanni Bottesini (1821-1889), the next famous bass virtuoso, refined solo technique and began writing more conjunct, lyrical passages in harmonics as well as the arpeggiated type of passagework, thus enlarging the scope and concept of writing in harmonics (Example 4).

Example 4: "Fantasia" from the Opera Lucia, Giovanni Bottesini

[3] Stylistically, this concerto is not like anything the celebrated "Paganini of the Double Bass" ever wrote. Unfortunately, it is on the same artistic level, and was probably written by E. Nanny, the noted pedagogue and contrabassist at the Paris Conservatory.

During Bottesini's lifetime the four-stringed contrabass became more popular and composers began to write for this instrument in Germany, France, and later in Italy. The noted
contrabassist, pedagogue, and composer Isaiah Bille began to promote the four-stringed
instrument and wrote études as well as other music for it. He even suggested employing
harmonics on all four strings! The following example is from one of his <u>Scherzi</u>.

Example 5: <u>Scherzo</u>, Isaiah Bille

Through the influence of Bille, the Italians developed a most refined technique of performing
harmonics which even included double-stopping. The next example is from Bille's <u>Organum</u>
and is written (in the unfortunate Italian tradition) at sounding pitch.

Example 6: <u>Organum</u>, Isaiah Bille

At this point in the development of this chapter it is necessary to discuss how and where to
play these harmonics. The Italian school tells us:

> All the harmonics given by the second half of the string, touched
> with sureness, have a splendid effect. It is well to use these al-
> most entirely, because they are stronger, more perfect in pitch
> and more beautiful. Those given by the first half, besides being
> less sure if the instrument is not more than perfect, are produced
> with difficulty and do not sound limpid; for this reason they must
> be rarely used and with great mastery, remembering to draw the
> bow always nearer the bridge — keeping it very light — while the
> left hand approaches the Capotasto. [4]

---

[4] From the preface to Bille, <u>Nuovo Method per Contrabasso</u>, Patre II (Milano, Ricordi:
1953) [not the first edition] •

Whereas the German school informs us:

> As these harmonics can also be produced in the lower position, I consider it of advantage to use these in preference to the others, in the first place as they are more convenient to stop and secondly as the fingers need not come in contact with the rosin which always settles on the strings near the bridge. [5]

Clearly the Italian and German schools have completely different ideas. Regarding the Italian method, I have made tape-recorded tests on several different basses to compare the strength (e.g., density and projection) and intonation of harmonics played on both halves, and find no significant difference. [6] The ease of production is a personal matter; many players feel more comfortable in the first half, and that's where they play most of the time. Thus it should be clear that harmonics on both halves of the string are feasible. The German school's admonition against playing "up in the rosin" is well taken. With the development of artificial harmonics, many of these notes are now playable with great ease, less body strain, and less rosin on the fingers. The matter of security is also a matter of personal taste; any supposed differences were not audible in the recorded tests.

The American school of contrabass performance has taken the best of these two schools, plus some ideas from the Spanish (the late Anton Torello, who taught at Curtis and played in the Philadelphia Orchestra), the English (the late Nelson Watson, who taught at Eastman and played in the Rochester Philharmonic, and the French schools), and tempered them with great pragmatism. The following passage from the distinguished American contrabassist and teacher Warren Benfield was an answer to one of my letters asking about harmonics: [7]

> I use the harmonics in both halves of the bass about equally. In Stravinsky, I use the first half of the string. For instance, I play the F♯ harmonic over the F♯, B over B, etc. I play the G harmonic over C. I do the same in Ravel, the first half of the string, even the high G over B♭. On some instances, I use artificial harmonics by placing the thumb on the middle of the string (harm.) and then graze the string over C to get 2 octaves higher and back over B to get the high B, etc. Most of the men in our section use this area to get those notes rather than the first half as I do. For solo playing, I usually use the second half of the string over the pressed note which would be the same. However, in the Hindemith Sonata, I again play the harmonics in the first half of the string. I suppose after 36 years of professional playing, I have gotten used to playing harmonics in the standard repertoire in my way and when new ones come up, I play them where they are most convenient after figuring what the hell the guy wanted, real sound or the way he has written them.

Many other performers take the approach described by Mr. Benfield, as I do also.

---

[5] Franz Simandl, New Method for the Double Bass (New York: Carl Fischer, Inc., 1958), p. 63. (A later translation of the original German publication.)

[6] Bille played on gut strings and we may surmise that his remarks are perfectly valid on these strings. The research for this book, however, has been done exclusively on steel strings and my results were quite different (in this case).

[7] Mr. Benfield is a member of the Chicago Symphony and teaches at De Paul and Northwestern Universities.

Simandl suggests that the following harmonics are available: [8]

Example 7: Simandl

In Examples 8 and 9 Simandl shows how to produce these with his two positions.

Example 8:

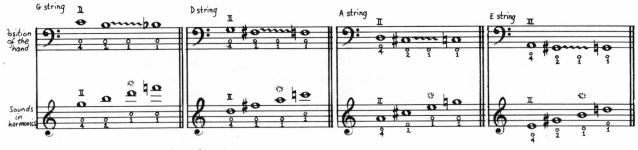

The harmonics marked ✳ must be stopped slightly higher than the natural tones in the hand position.

---

[8] Franz Simandl, <u>New Method for the Double Bass</u> (New York: Carl Fischer, Inc., 1948), Vol. 2.

Example 9:

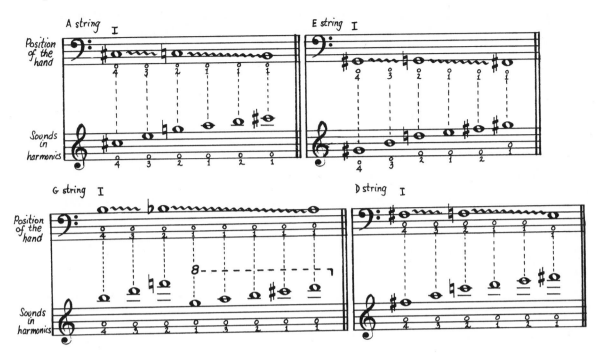

Bille offers a table for available natural harmonics also.

Example 10: Isaiah Bille

Note that the German school is now also mistaken, as is the Italian school (Bille on the best place to play harmonics) as to the problem of playing harmonics above the third octave on the first half of the string. This is enormously difficult, bordering on the impossible. It is possible sometimes on the first and second strings, but out of the question on the A and E strings.

After a decade of working on harmonics and consulting many bassists and composers, I offer the following ideas about where to play the harmonics. The obvious answer, of course, is "wherever you are most comfortable." But let us start after that concept as it is usually influenced by training and not by personal choice.

I suggest playing natural harmonics "in the positions" or on the first half of the fingerboard. The sound and its color and projection are the same on any fine instrument with sensitive strings and a good "setup." The playing positions (i.e., the first half of the fingerboard) are best known to the largest majority of players and therefore (with practice) should be easier and safer to use for passagework in harmonics.[9] The harmonics up to the flat seventh and third octave can be handled quite accurately, as may be seen in Example 8. The following virtuosic examples (11-15) from Lawrence Moss's Windows (1966) might appear beyond the resources of the contrabass; however, played "in the positions" it becomes an excellent example of idiomatic writing for the instrument.

Example 11:

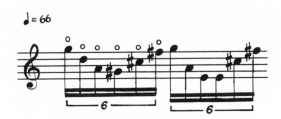

Example 12:

In twentieth century music, with abrupt disjunct motion as a norm, passages such as Example 13 becomes most difficult if played in the style of the Italian school, as opposed to the simplicity of ease of performance using the German method.

---

[9] I should also like to add "comfort," as you don't have to lean over the end of the fingerboard and hurt your back while getting your fingers all rosined up for no apparent reason!

Example 13:

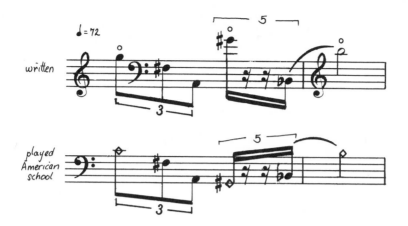

The choreography required to perform this brief excerpt with the harmonics at the upper half of the fingerboard would be Olympian, and, after testing many professional colleagues, I can safely report it still unplayable!

Let us go back to Example 13 and amplify the playing position concept. If the second octave, third, and fifth are played 4, 2, 1, then the hand position could also be moved up to give the third, fifth, and seventh.

Example 14:

And once again to get the fifth, seventh, and third octave. (This is precarious and requires much practice and a lot of luck!)

Example 15:

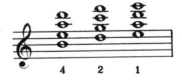

Natural harmonics above the third octave are rarely called for and more rarely heard. If such a pitch is written it usually can be handled with ease and security by an artificial harmonic.

The following example from the twentieth century literature is conceived (by the composer) to be played in the first half of the fingerboard. The example from <u>Recitative and Aria for Solo Contrabass</u> (1964) by Allen Hoffman is a lovely lyric passage that "lies in the hand" except for two simple shifts to G:

Example 16: Recitative and Aria for Solo Contrabass (1964), Allen Hoffman

A passage of such lyric character is a travesty unless the performer colors it (with regis-
tration-bow placement, see Chapter II) and "warms it up" with vibrato. There is no reason
but unquestioned tradition for the natural harmonics to be only a white, dead sound! If this
is not the composer's intention then the performer must play harmonics in the musical context. [10] I bring this point out since harmonics usually are played very poorly. To close
this digression about the musicality of performance of natural harmonics, let me add that
crescendo and diminuendo are possible and necessary and can be controlled easily by the
weight and speed of the bow.

In the 1960's I came upon "pulled harmonics," a technique that can raise all the natural
harmonics a microtone, a semitone, or even more according to the amount of tension on the
string resulting from pulling it to the side at the node of the harmonic. This technique is
idiomatic to the blues guitarist, and I first saw and heard its transformation to the contrabass one evening at a Charles Mingus performance. Pulled harmonics are notated P↗[11] and
can be used to color pitches microtonally, to create a "frequency flux" (—wa — wa — wa), or
to produce eight separate overtone series instead of the standard four. Their fundamentals
are E, F, A, Bb, D, Eb, G, and Ab. These "new" overtones take preparation and work
well up to at least the second fifth on all four strings. Also, pulled harmonics can clear up
some intonation problems, especially if the bass is flat, as well as open up a veritable
cosmos of natural harmonics. [12]

Barney Childs makes use of pulled harmonics in the bass solo from the slow movement of
his Quartet for Flute, Oboe, Percussion and Bass (1964) (Example 17).

---

[10] If the composer wants the white dead sound, he should indicate it.

[11] Courtesy of Barney Childs, 1964. The symbol is a combination of a P for "pizzicato"
and an arrow for "up."

[12] George Perle plays off the intonation differences between G as the octave on the G
string and G as the seventh of the string — also the same with D (II and IV) in Monody II
(1962).

Example 17: <u>Quartet for Flute, Oboe, Percussion and Bass</u> (1964), Barney Childs

E. J. Miller, in the "Study for String Bass Harmonics" (1964) was asked to restrict himself to the use of natural harmonics only, and within these restrictions used doublestop harmonics including some large stretches for the first time.

Example 18:

The entire piece is playable with careful preparation and constitutes a musical thesaurus of natural harmonics.

At this point a comment on notation is in order. I should like to suggest the following: Because the contrabass is a transposing instrument all harmonics should be notated an octave higher than the desired pitch, in the treble clef, with the conventional harmonic symbol "o". The ridiculously confusing practice of indicating the string, finger placement, actual sounds, etc., should be abolished, as it clutters up the printed page and purveys confusion, not information. Thus, I would prefer notation for contrabass to be consistently transposing an octave lower than written despite the verbiage in orchestration books and the unquestioned tradition of notation still passed on in some music centers of the world.

Kenneth Winstead, prominent Los Angeles teacher and performer, wrote to me: "If a bassist is competent enough to execute harmonics, he will know where to find them." An excellent example of the dangers of the tablature notation is the passage in Movement 1 of the Sonata for Double Bass and Piano (1949) by Paul Hindemith, where the tablature calls for excessive shifting. The purpose of tablature is to guide the performer to the most convenient, colorful, safe, or easiest fingering, and clearly this is not the case with Hindemith's instructions. It must be said, to present both sides of the story, that some bassists still prefer the tablature. It is my distinct feeling that with some new solo literature and études using harmonics the technique will become a sine qua non and the tablature will vanish since crutches will no longer be needed.

Artificial harmonics have not found much prominence in the solo and chamber music literature of the contrabass at this writing. My remark in 1967, "Most solo bassists have mastered the necessary technique," [13] was more optimistic than realistic. The reason for writing this was my nonacceptance of the idea that a technique must often be used, taught, and practiced before being employed by serious composers. Techniques get into the mainstream of enlightened instrumentalism only when they are used in printed music with wide circulation. Since my article was basically for composers I felt this posture would help the situation along. In 1970 artificial harmonics are still not in the mainstream. It is my fervent hope that the exposition to follow will solve problems and answer questions for composers, performers, and interested musicians and thus change the "bias" toward artificial harmonics.

Our discussion on this subject will, of necessity, be of a technical nature and will not be graced by a historical introduction.

The feasibility of artificial harmonics generally has to do with the length of the string, the length and breadth of the player's hand, and the preparation time before the note is played. The adoption of steel strings has increased the ease of production of artificial harmonics and, in fact, looking back to the era of the physical and acoustical properties of gut, both Bille and Simandl suggested only the use of the first string to produce artificial harmonics.[14] Today, with steel strings used by the large majority of bassists, artificial harmonics are available on all four strings.[15]

---

[13] "Notes on the Double Bass," Source (Jan. 1967).

[14] Bille tells us that artificial harmonics on other strings "are perfectly useless" and Simandl insinuates these sentiments as his examples only use the first string.

[15] Henry Portnoi (Boston Symphony) and Professor Eldon Obrecht (University of Iowa) suggest that artificial harmonics on the E string constitute a special effect due to the rich and "foggy" sound produced.

The most important things to know about artificial harmonics are these:

1. They are available on all strings.

2. Artificial harmonics with the fourth and fifth stopped should begin only on or above the minor seventh from the open string. The harmonic using the third is usuable in lower positions (depending on the hand of the performer) beginning in the second position. That is, I = Bb, II = F, III = C, and IV = G.

3. Use of the thumb pressing the string down with the second (or third) finger lightly stopping the fifth above will obtain the fifth an octave higher (see Example 19).

Example 19:

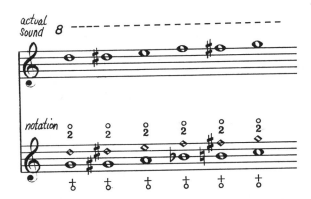

Use of the same position with the fourth stopped produces the fundamental two octaves higher.

Example 20:

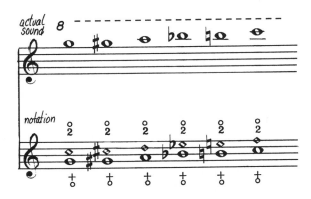

Stopping the third produces the third two octaves higher.

Example 21:

This is basically factual data, important for the composer and performer to know about artificial harmonics, presented hopefully in a clear, concise manner. Before closing I should like to point out that most contrabasses have a B or C (sounding above middle C) as the final highest stopped note. To facilitate writing or playing a chromatic scale a combination of the three positions should be used thus:

Example 22:

CODA

1. A most interesting effect is produced by a glissando in artificial harmonics without adjusting the hand position as you move up and down. The descending glissando, with the many breaks, resembles a sea gull call.

Example 23:

2. All the natural harmonics are available pizzicato and col legno battuto. Some of the pizzicato harmonics might be best produced with fingernail pizzicato or quasi-ponticello registration. Bow placement in col legno battuto is sometimes critical, and projection is best attained by striking near the bridge.

3. When you stop a string, touch the next octave with your right hand thumb and pluck; the result is a harmonic one octave higher than the stopped note. This technique was adopted from jazz guitar by bassist Alan Goldman and demonstrated to Barney Childs in 1967. The first appearance of the pizzicato artificial harmonic in printed music was in Mr. T., His Fancy (1967) by Barney Childs. In November 1970, composer guitarist Allen Strange and I did some research into the potential of this technique. After some time, we discovered that by using the thumb and the first finger plucking the string simultaneously, the fundamental and the octave can be sounded. Conversely, when repeating this process

on the third a tenth fundamental is sounded, on the fifth a twelfth fundamental, and on the
second octave a double octave. The other overtones simply don't work. The sound of these
harmonics, playing single notes and double stops, is very clear, projected, and similar to
a harp harmonic. As this technique is still in the laboratory stage a notation has not yet
been worked out. Perhaps I could suggest this notation as a stopgap:

Example 24:

The effect is, in fact, an artificial harmonic; therefore, the conventional artificial harmonic notation seems appropriate. However, the octave (or any other overtone) node is
stopped with a finger or thumb of the right hand so this should also be evident in the notation.
The solution would then seem to be a pizzicato indication of the node pitch with a line connect-
ing the pizzicato sign and the node indication. The line also gives a graphic representation
of the use of the two fingers of the right hand (the thumb touching the node and plucking with
the index finger).

4. I have (frequently) been asked by many composers to list which harmonics speak well
and to discuss their sonorous characteristics, as well as the preparation time necessary for
the production of some artificial harmonics. These answers are out of the range of this
book and depend, in most cases, on the individual performer, his instrument and its "setup"
and strings, the acoustical environment, and the musical context. Problems such as the
preparation time needed to produce artificial harmonics will be solved in the years to come
provided they are used by composers, insisted on by conductors, and taught by enlightened
instrumentalists.

Example 25:

Chapter VI: Miscellanea

This chapter has functioned as somewhat of a catchall since the inception of this book. It is the home of ideas of a noncategorical nature and those on the fringe, as well as speculations about the potential usage and juxtaposition of some techniques. Although some of the material is articulated in print for the first time, it is my idea to stimulate, not to codify. It is my fervent hope that these ideas open doors to new sound worlds for composers and performers.

SCORDATURA

Scordatura has been an idiomatic technique since the inception of contrabass playing. The three-string bassists in the eighteenth and early nineteenth century changed their tuning to fit the composition being performed and alternated between G-D-A, A-D-G, G-D-G, or A-D-A. The first famous contrabass virtuoso, Domenico Dragonetti (1763-1846), was known to be a master of scordatura. Adjustment of tuning was used by some composers and performers for more than ease: their concern was with projection and what was considered a more soloistic sound. The changed sound of the contrabass tuned up a semitone or whole tone (or up to a fourth with "high" solo strings) has more "edge" and, in fact, a brilliance not unlike a cello.

This tradition has been kept alive mainly by the European publishers, composers, and pedagogues, and the international set of performers who are still integrally committed to keeping the eighteenth- and nineteenth-century solo literature, such as it is, within earshot. It is my contention that this tradition has value but can no longer be seriously considered as the only approach to soloism.

Scordatura has been used by twentieth-century composers primarily in two ways: (1) The E (fourth string) has been lowered to Eb, D, Db, or C for extension of the lower range, although below D the string gets flabby and does not sound well. A solution I have used with much success is to employ a C string for the fourth (i.e., E) string. This tuning/stringing is called for in De Profundis (1960) by Ralph Shapey and Charles Wuorinen's Concert for

Double Bass Alone (1961). (2) Scordatura is employed when the composer needs various harmonics playable on a higher or lower string. George Crumb lowers the fourth string to Eb for this purpose in his Book I Madrigals (1965) for soprano, vibraphone, and contrabass.

John Cage has employed a constantly-changing scordatura in the "Solo for Bass" from the Concert for Piano and Orchestra (1957-1958) and other works. This affects the sound of the instrument, as the pressure on the bridge is constantly being changed, as well as bringing about microtonal coloration.

A very interesting scordatura is called for by Alcides Lanza in Strobo I (1968). The top two strings are tuned as high as possible while three and four are tuned as low as possible.

Jazz bassists in the 1950's had a fad going with a C, G, D, A tuning. This had its origins, most probably, with the vogue of "Chubby" Jackson, who actually had the Kay Company build some five-string basses with the high C as the fifth string. The excellence of high register solo playing and the new desire of today's composers to use all registers of the instrument has dampened the enthusiasm of these experimenters and little has been heard about this idea for some time.

MUTES

Most composers have notions about what muted string instruments sound like, but are they aware of the different materials mutes are made of and their resultant sound? Few composers are cognizant of this and can only recall composing for a specific type of mute. Arnold Franchetti grew fond of a brass mute he heard used in a chamber music performance in the late 1950's and often calls for metal mute in his scores (both orchestral and chamber).

At this writing I know of only one composer who has made use of the different timbres available from various mutes. John Cage, in his Concert for Piano and Orchestra (1957-1958), asks the bassist for three different types of mutes. He doesn't specify the material; so, although asking for timbral differentiation, he doesn't specify precisely what these niceties should be.

In these days when timbre is so important, it would seem appropriate to investigate the potential of various mutes and use it compositionally.

At this writing I am in possession of brass, rosewood, hard rubber, and plastic mutes. The recording accompanying this book has a band dealing with these four different mutes. In the future I hope to find leather, ebony, and aluminum mutes and experiment further.

This brief exposition on muting may sound far-fetched to the musician who has lived in the orchestral jungle and seen/heard the Mahler First Symphony solo performed without a mute, or other such markings overlooked in Debussy, Ravel, early Stravinsky and many others. This type of antimusical behavior is less tolerated by conductors these days and in no way should reflect on the music-making of bassists in the very near future.

GLISSANDI

I. Generators:

   1. pizzicato (guitar, normal)

   2. slap pizzicato

   3. pizzicato tremolo

   4. arco

   5. arco tremolo

   6. col legno battuto or a dowel, pencil, vibe mallet

   7. col legno tratto

II. Techniques that sustain the glissando in motion:

   1. pizzicato tremolo

   2. arco (with any registration)

   3. arco tremolo

   4. col legno battuto tremolo

   5. col legno tratto

   6. col legno tratto tremolo

III. A glissando can consist of:

   1. one note, stopped or harmonic, played ordinario or with a trill

   2. a double stop, stopped or harmonics, played ordinario or with trills.

   3. three or four notes if it is a strum (pizzicato tremolo) glissando

IV. Some glissandi change generators after they are initiated:

   1. a pizzicato glissando may change to arco midway

   2. an arco glissando may change to pizzicato tremolo

   3. a col legno battuto glissando may change to arco or pizzicato tremolo midway

   4. a pizzicato tremolo glissando may change to arco

   5. an arco glissando may change to a pizzicato tremolo

   6. an arco tremolo glissando may change to pizzicato tremolo

   7. a pizzicato tremolo glissando may change to an arco tremolo glissando

   8. a pizzicato-activated glissando changes to arco briefly, then the bow is removed and the glissando continued

V. Glissando from open E string down to a rumble:

   1. Richard Moryl — Systems (1969)

      2. Donald Erb — <u>In No Strnge Land</u> (1968)

VI. Vocal sounds can be used with glissandi very effectively in two ways:

      1. in parallel motion to reinforce, amplify, or modulate

      2. in contrary motion

For ponticello glissandi, vocal sounds with predominant <u>s</u> sounds (like "shoosh," hiss, or "shhh") produce the most effective mix, either (1) or (2).

MIXES

There are basically two categories of mixes:

I. Two-part:

      A. arco-vocal

          arco-percussive

          arco-pizzicato

          arco-rub

      B. pizzicato-vocal

          pizzicato-percussive

          pizzicato-rub

      C. percussive-vocal

      D. l. h. alone-vocal

          l. h. alone-rub

          l. h. alone-percussive

          l. h. alone-pizzicato

          l. h. alone-arco, and

II. Three part:

      A. arco-vocal-percussive

          arco-vocal-rub

          arco-vocal-pizzicato

          arco-vocal-l. h. alone

      B. pizzicato-vocal-rub

          pizzicato-vocal-percussive

          pizzicato-vocal-l. h. alone

In <u>Phantasmagoria</u> (1968) by Wayne Peterson there are several examples of slap pizzicato reinforced by knuckle or palm slap, an excellent mix with great projection. Another interesting two-part mix utilizing percussion is found in John Mizelle's <u>Degree of Change</u> (1967) in which he uses pairs of two dichotomous elements — the left hand knocking on the

shoulder of the bass in accelerando and diminuendo, while the right hand bows low E's,
crescendo and ritardando.

Example 1: <u>Degree of Change</u> (1967), John Mizelle

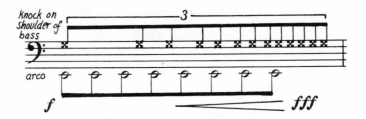

In the <u>Color Studies</u> (1969) by Jon Deak we find a very delicate two-part mix comprised
of left hand pizzicato over vertical bowing at the side of the bridge.

Example 2: <u>Color Studies</u>, Jon Deak

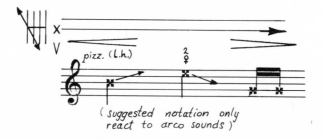

A veritable arsenal of two-part mixes are found in <u>Triplicity</u> (1970) by Jogi Yuasa.
The first mix is comprised of contrabass tones masked by bowed tam-tam sounds on tape.
These tones are sustained normally as well as tremolando.   Ponticello is a natural mix
for bowed gongs, especially when the bow is so close to the bridge as to produce clusters
of random harmonics.   This area is another lacuna that calls for more exploration.

Other notable two-part mixes include (1) the use of the tailpiece struck with a vibe
mallet, coupled with various strings struck below the bridge; (2) the tailpiece coupled with
the palm on the bass body (also possible, but not used by Yuasa, are the coupling with the
four other percussion generators discussed in Chapter III); and (3) the palm on the waist
of the bass mixed with a string struck behind the bridge.   The various parts of the instrument's body struck by the other four generators would also provide excellent mixes
with the behind-the-bridge stringwork.   The click tongue makes an excellent resonant
sound and is used by Yuasa in the very colorful cadenza section.   In this same section he

colors arco harmonics with vocal sounds and uses the fluttertongues to color knuckle percussive effects. And finally, over a fluttertongue drone, the composer writes a short pizzicato passage, bringing to mind many such vocal drones that could be the undergirding of innumerable arco-pizzicato-percussive passages or mixtures of these techniques.

Inside (1969) by Kenneth Gaburo is a major source of vocal and instrumental mixes. I list a selection of his two-part mixes to conclude this section.

1.   Glissando activated with a vocal sound

2.   Vocal sound mixed with ponticello tremolo

3.   Contrabass trill plus voice waver (undulation)

4.   Various phonemes with different percussion sounds

5.   Four-part chord in harmonics strummed with the thumb

     mixed with a vocal crescendo on various phonemes

     taken from the title

6.   Molto vibrato bass note, arco, plus a fluttered r which

     changes into a sucking sound

7.   Bass sul ponticello (tremolo or up bow) plus vocal

     kissing sound (single or repeated)

8.   Vocal sound plus arco legato col legno, bridge to

     fingerboard, plus pitch

9.   Wavering pulled harmonic plus vocal sound

10.   Finger snap plus vocal sound

11.   Vocal sound plus col legno, bounce on strings plus pitch

12.   Vocal sound plus heel of bow on tailpiece

13.   Vocal sound plus high trill.

Musical examples for all are in Example 3.

Example 3: <u>Inside</u> (1969), Kenneth Gaburo

glissando activated with a vocal sound

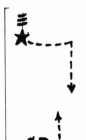

vocal sound mixed with ponticello tremolo

contrabass trill plus voice waver

various phonemes with different percussion sounds

four-part chord in harmonics strummed with the thumb
mixed with a vocal crescendo on various phonemes taken
from the title

motto vibrato bass note, arco, plus a fluttered "R"
which changes into a sucking sound

Example 3: (continued)

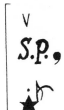

bass sul ponticello (tremolo or up bow) plus vocal kissing sound (single or repeated)

vocal sound plus arco legato col legno, bridge to fingerboard, plus pitch

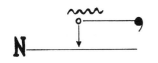

wavering pulled harmonic plus vocal sound

M
X

finger snap plus vocal sound

vocal sound plus col legno, bounce on strings plus pitch

T.P.

vocal sound plus heel of bow on tailpiece

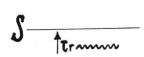

vocal sound plus high trill

The area of the three-part mix is very special and exotic, but capable of producing some very elegant and complex textures. Jogi Yuasa uses a two-part mix (referred to on page as #1) supplemented by a sound described as an "explosive sound with lips, just like the sound uncorking the bottle." Again I should like to point out that this mix would also be colored and articulated beautifully by the host of other vocal sounds at our disposal.

There are two most complicated three-part mixes in Gaburo's <u>Inside</u> (1969). The first consists of a vocal sound plus arco <u>col legno legato</u> (with pitch-l.h.) plus a cupped hand on the bass shoulder. The second consists of the heel of the bow on the tailpiece plus a fingertip on the shoulder topped off by a vocal sound.

Jon Deak concludes his study of De Chirico's "The Two Sisters" (from his <u>Surrealist Studies</u> [1970]) with the following spectacular three-part mix:

Example 4: <u>Surrealist Studies</u> (1970), Jon Deak

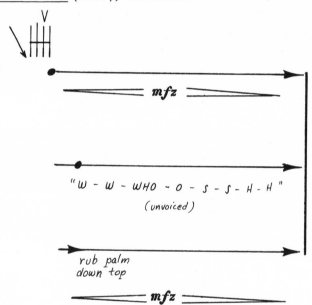

I should like to conclude this section of three-part mixes with a mini-catalogue of possible mix components:

A. Vocal sounds:

    1. whsssh (exhaling)

    2. his

    3. talking

    4. whispering

    5. any other colorful or expressive vocal sounds

B. Arco/pizzicato:

    1. arco

    2. arco tremolando / any different registrations

    3. pizzicato

4. guitar pizzicato
5. pizzicato tremolo
6. left hand pizzicato
7. left hand alone
8. bi-tone pizzicato

C. Percussion sounds:

1. The generators are fingertip, fingernail, palm, knuckle, or cupped hand, and they can be played on the back, front, shoulder, tailpiece, bridge, and scroll of the bass.

I should like to point out that four-part mixes are possible and have been used, and as I write these words several five-part mixes come to my inner ear. Because I said I wish to open the doors and suggest ideas and also because this area of mixes is most complicated already up to three-part, I will close the discussion at this point.

This section is reinforced, amplified, and perhaps interpreted by the accompanying long playing record. It seems that some of these sound complexes presented, discussed, or speculated upon will be of much use and interest to composers and performers, as they parallel the multiphonic revolution currently going on in the world of the woodwind and brass instruments.

Chapter VII: Amplification and Electronic Effects

A book on new timbral resources for a stringed instrument written in the 1970's would be incomplete without a discussion of amplification and electronics. As this area is far afield for me, a uniquely qualified writer has been enlisted. Mr. Arnold Lazarus, president of the Strobtronix Corporation of San Francisco, is an inventive physicist as well as a trained musician. His outstanding work and deep concern and commitment to music made it clear that he should be the author of this chapter.

To conclude this brief introduction I should like to point out that this chapter is primarily designed for the performer, whereas the other six chapters are constructed for both composer and performer.

PHILOSOPHICAL AND REALISTIC CONSIDERATIONS

Amplify: 1. To make larger or stronger, increase or extend

2. To strengthen (electrical impulses) by means of electronic tubes, etc. — Webster's New World Dictionary

Virtually every bassist today is familiar with some phase of electronic amplification whether it be his stereo set or the amplification system for his bass. Even if he never uses an "amp" he cannot avoid some contact with electronic effects — almost every record made today uses some form or another. It may be an echo, frequency compensation, of any one of the many forms of effects available. Although the sound will eventually emanate from a speaker system at an increased volume, one must distinguish between amplification and electronic effects yet realize that they work together. The important thing is to know what one wants. If an exact reproduction of the original tones is desired, theoretically the same tones that go into an amplification system must come out of it — only louder. This is consistent with the definition of <u>amplify</u>. Yet because of pickup, microphone, speakers, or room acoustics pure amplification may be impossible and additional effects may be required to simulate the actual tones. If the simulation cannot be detected by the listener then it is successful.

This is a fully realistic concept. If, for example, one wishes increased bass or treble then he gets into amplified effects. These concepts are important as many musicians, both performing and recording artists, are today faced with a vast array of electronic equipment. The studio musician encounters microphones, tape recorders, mixers, etc. The performer is faced with similar equipment but must be forced to hear himself. The symphonic musician has the anxiety that he might encounter microphones or pickups at a live concert; or, in some cases, he fears that when he plays he cannot be heard without amplifications. [1]

The reasons for an amplified concert go back to the age when the only place to hear a concert was the village square (perhaps a traveling troubadour or the forerunner of a "festival"), salons, or theaters. As music grew, so did the number of people who wanted to experience the live performance. First the instruments underwent changes to permit soloists to be heard above the ensemble — an excellent example of this is the way the violin acquired the high bridge and longer fingerboard. Next came the concept that there is volume in large numbers — thus evolved the symphony orchestra.

Yet the man who sits in the first row gets a different experience from the man in the last row, and not necessarily a better one. What would be the result, then, if through tasteful and excellent amplification the man in front, back, or anywhere could hear a concert equally well? How many people go to a great concert and cannot hear a thing? And how much louder can we get by just adding more basses? It's even more frustrating when you read the reviews in the morning after the concert you went to but could not hear! Yet more people than ever before want the live performance. Look at the attendance at various coliseums, festivals, orchestral performances, and dance concerts. The only answer is good quality amplification which, incidentally, has an interesting history of its own.

Quality amplification has grown greatly in the past four years, as has power usage. The famous Fillmore/West in San Francisco began with four mikes and 160 watts of power. They now have 30 mike lines, 16 mikes, and 1200 watts, a power increase in four years of 8 to 1. The hall size has remained the same, so why the power gain? The answer is dispersion. They can now reach more people more evenly and give a smoother performance. This does not mean that more power automatically means a better concert, but speaker

---

[1] At the International Bass Workshop (Los Angeles, June 1970) Gary Karr said that he felt there was a good possibility that orchestral bass sections would eventually be amplified in order to meet the growing demands for live performances.

placement and sound dispersion do contribute to it. At the present time sound still emanates from the stage in most concerts but ideally an even blanket of sound should be placed on an audience. At the present time this technique is difficult: since sound travels relatively slowly and different sounds reach various parts of the room at different times, delay systems are needed. But, I strongly feel that this system will be achieved successfully in the near future.

The rock musicians and the electronic music composers use amplification to an extreme in the sense of effects and volume level, but as high power PA (public address) systems become more sophisticated and are able to produce high quality sound amplification the musical community is beginning to anticipate the day when virtually every performance would include amplification — be it classical, jazz, rock, or any other kind of music — but with taste and balance. A new group of electronically and musically oriented engineers, who do the mixing and control the amplification of the performance, is beginning to evolve and work more closely with the performers than ever before. As Rich McKean of the Fillmore/ West says, "We want to strive to make the hall sound just as the musicians think they sound." With this concept in mind along with that of the original high fidelity (recreate the concert hall) concept, let us look further into the logical reasons, the fears, and the implications of amplified performances in relation to the bass.

There are three basic methods of approaching the problem of working with electronic amplification of your instrument. The first is to buy equipment from a dealer, read the instructions, and hope for the best. The second is to learn as much as possible about audio amplification, select carefully the best equipment you can afford for your instrument, and spend a great deal of time and study learning to use it for optimum results in relation to your tasks. The third, which is quite widely practiced now among rock musicians, is to find an "audio man" to take care of your sound. The first and third methods have two things in common: they will not give the musician complete control over his facilities because of lack of knowledge and control, and they will rarely optimize the sound because of a lack of interest and responsibility.

The key word is <u>responsibility</u>. A person has a responsibility to himself and his audience to get the best sound possible with his equipment. If an audio man is required, and in recording studios, then the musician must work intimately with him and in actuality dictate what kind of sound he wants. The second method is the most versatile, has the most control, and will generally get the best results. You must learn about electronics with the same zeal you would learn to play a new bass. Electronic amplification must be approached in the same manner. Experiment and learn what your sound system can do and cannot do. Electronics should not only become a new instrument to be studied and mastered but also an extension of your own musical personality.

AMPLIFYING THE BASS

    The basic amplification system is illustrated in Figure 1. It consists of a source (pickup or microphone), preamplifier, electronics effects control center, power amplifier, and speaker system. Each unit will be described in this section so that the reader will have a working familiarity with a basic amplification system. The basic system will always be the same despite the configuration, whether there are separate power supplies for each stage or one master supply for all stages of amplification.

Figure 1.

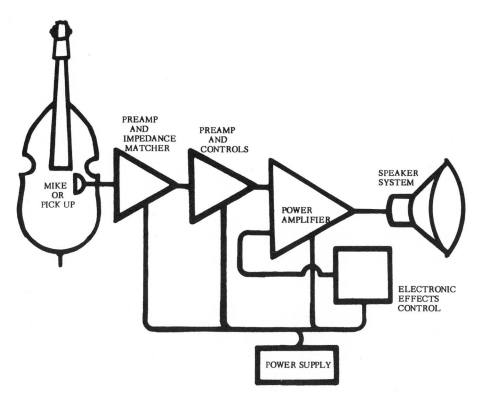

A. The pickup: There are two basic methods of bass amplification — the pickup, such as the FRAP (Flat Response Audio Pickup) and microphones,which include the contact mike. Both feed into amplifier-speaker systems. The main differences between them are frequency response and isolation. The microphones available are of a huge variety both in style (dynamic, condenser, crystal) and price range (from $1. 99 to approximate $300. 00). The problems with microphones are basically simple: they will pick up other instruments, their frequency response leaves much to be desired for bass reproduction (although the more expensive ones will do the job quite well), there is feedback, and placement is difficult (they must be placed in relation to the bass and this placement varies from room to room and from instrument to instrument). Thus a mike is highly inconvenient for the bassist who plays under a variety of conditions.

The pickups available are of two basic types — magnetic and piezoelectric. Both afford isolation from picking up other sounds. The magnetic pickup is basically a coil wound around a magnet. Then a metallic object such as a string moves near it a voltage is generated proportional to the movement of the object, which in this case is the string. This is the type of pickup used on most electric guitars and basses. The main disadvantage of this pickup is that, although you pay a great deal for a carefully designed wooden sound wave shaper, i.e., the bass, the magnetic pickup will not pick up the reflected sound of the bass, only of the strings. That is why a bass with a magnetic pickup sounds very similar to an electric bass. Another major drawback of the magnetic pickup is that it is fixed in position; as you move down the fingerboard the proximity of the string to the magnet changes and so does the volume, with as much unevenness of tone. Because of its inherent design, the magnetic pickup is very susceptible to picking up both 60 and 120 Hz induced hum. A good example of the many magnetic pickups on the market is the TOBE.

The finest pickup, in terms of frequenty response, isolation, evenness of tone, and lack of feedback, is the piezoelectric pickup such as the FRAP or BARCUS-BERRY. The piezoelectric device is nonmagnetic and thus relatively hum-free. Its frequency response potential is the widest of all, ranging from a few Hz to over 100,000 Hz, depending upon its design. It has no moving parts and has extremely fast transient response, so when a flurry of fast notes and sharp sforzandos must be played each note can be heard perfectly and cleanly. This pickup works on the principle that as a piece of piezoelectric material is deformed, a voltage is produced. If it can be deformed by the vibrations of a musical instrument, and a proportional voltage created, then we can amplify these vibrations. Piezoelectric units are of two basic types — fixed position, such as the BARCUS-BERRY, and movable, such as the FRAP. Fixed position pickups are generally located in the vicinity of the bridge and pick up a maximum of the string tone, but since the bridge is theoretically a relatively toneless transducer (which transmits the string sound to the instrument and then to the ear) we hear mainly the string tone rather than the tone shaped by the body of the bass. The time this takes, the response time, makes instruments sound either sluggish or crisp. Because of the unit's fixed location on or under the bridge it does not pick up a maximum of the acoustic sound of the bass, much like the magnetic pickup, and it has a tendency to pick up the string noise as well. Also the fixed position pickup cannot account for a difference in instruments.

The movable type of pickup is by far the most versatile in the potential of effects and adaption to any instrument. The FRAP,[2] for example, is attached to the instrument with an

---

[2] The FRAP, incidentally, has a frequency response of 5 to 100,000 Hz, thus enabling the subharmonic structure of the tone to be amplified. Subharmonics are important as they reinforce the fundamentals just as harmonics do. They follow the sequence fo/2, fo/3, etc., where fo is the fundamental and fo/2 is the first subharmonic, fo/3 the record, etc.

adhesive wax and can be placed or moved anywhere on the instrument in seconds. For a blunt, electronic pizzicato you can place it on the scroll. For a rich dark sound, the back or bass bar is excellent. For a harsh cutting sound, use the bridge area. The variety of timbres available offers composer and performer tremendous potential.

Selection of a good pickup and speaker system depends much upon personal tastes, but amplifier selection is quite cut and dried. Virtually all the high quality amplifiers are good and you only have to select for your power requirements, desired effects, and reliability.

B. Preamplifier: The signal produced by the pickup on the instrument is too weak to be accurately boosted by the power amplifier (see F). One of the functions of the preamplifier is to raise the signal to such a level that it may be accurately operated on by the power amplifier — hence, the term preamplifier. In order to prevent any loss in power or adverse effects to the frequency response, the preamplifier also performs the functions of impedance matching and providing control over the tone. Impedance matching is analogous to fitting water pipes of the same diameter together to prevent spillage. When one has two pipes of different diameters and wants to connect them, he obtains an adaptor which has the two diameters of the respective pipes. In electronics the preamplifier performs the function of impedance matching (the adaptor) to prevent loss of signal.

C. Tone controls: In every modern amplification system bass and treble controls are usually included as part of the preamplifier circuit. The function of these controls is to amplify or attenuate the bass or treble region or both simultaneously. Not only can one compensate for a room's acoustics with these controls, but the tone of his instrument can be changed electronically through their use. Other types of tone controls are called equalizers, which operate in such a manner as to shape the tone of a particular frequency range. The most sophisticated tone control system divides the audio spectrum into many bands and offers a control that boosts or attenuates each band; this is likely to be found in recording systems or big PA systems.

As with any tool, the tone controls must be used artistically. It is extremely important to know how one's particular controls work in their relative positions in order to obtain the desired amplified sound. The musician must be many times more aware of his controls than the owner of a stereo set.

D. Electronic Effects:
　　　　1. Tremolo
　　　　2. Vibrato
　　　　3. Echo and reverberation
　　　　4. Fuzz
　　　　5. Wah-wah

6. Tone extenders

7. Electronic music systems

Electronic effects present an entirely new set of dimensions to the sound of an instrument. However, successful use of these effects depends entirely on the taste and sensitivity of the performer and his equipment. One must think of them as the spices of amplification. The effects presented in this section are by now means complete, and as of this printing much that is new is being developed.

1. The tremolo is basically a variation in volume level which ranges in rates of 1 Hz (formally, cycles per second or cps) to 14 or 15 Hz. As the lowest frequency on the four-stringed bass (e) is approximately 40 Hz, this variance would be almost inaudible in the lowest range of the bass until notes around 250 Hz are played. To use this on bass would therefore take careful and thoughtful experimentation. The tremolo controls will generally be strength (amplitude) and speed (frequency).

2. An electronic vibrato circuit produces a periodic variation in the frequency or pitch of the input signal. Like the tremolo, the rate of frequency change may be varied over a range of about 1 Hz to 14 or 15 Hz. In an attempt to simulate manually produced vibrato the degree of frequency change is very small, usually not exceeding a quarter tone. On more complex circuits the amount of frequency deviation, technically referred to as "index," may be varied to produce many fascinating effects. Unfortunately this circuit is a luxury found on the more sophisticated systems and the performer usually has to be content with the availability of tremolo.

3. Echo or reverberation is another effect that, like the tremolo, is difficult for the bassist, since it sounds better in the higher frequency range. An echo effect is obtained by taking off a part of the signal, delaying it slightly, and then adding it to the original signal. The original note sounds, and a fraction of a second later there is an echo. If the echoes are so close together that the listener can't separate them, the sound is called reveberation. The only difference between echo and reverberation is the length of time or amount of delay between the signals. Typical delay times are 29 and 37 milliseconds (1 millisecond equals 0.001 seconds), but not more than 50 milliseconds of the effect is to be classified as reverberation.

4. Fuzz sounds just as it implies. The sound is distorted and unclear.

5. Wah-wah is an electronic device that gives a sound based on the note or chord played, but with the effect that it sounds like "wah-wah." Technically speaking, this device is a

very sharp cutoff low pass filter.

6. In recent years the tone extender, also referred to as a sustain control, expander, or AGC (automatic gain control), has received great popularity with contemporary guitarists — it is also applicable to the bass. With the incorporation of this circuit any plucked or bowed note will sustain at a present level, thereby drastically extending the normal delay time. Depending on the sensitivity settings the sustain period may range from a normal delay to an infinite length of time.

7. With the advent of such electronic music synthesizers as MOOG, ARP, PUTNEY, ELECTROCOMP, and LUDWIG PHASE III, the musician is exposed to an entirely new tool and an opportunity to create sounds and effects that were previously limited by the output of his individual instrument. Although the systems mentioned above are basically for the keyboard-oriented performer, there are some methods of plugging in a source from instruments, such as a bass, by using a pickup or a microphone. The Parasound Corporation is currently prototyping a mini-system that will be primarily for string players. This can shape the tones to any extent that the musician desires and introduce any set of overtones and proportions derived. This will finally give the string-oriented person an opportunity to play with electronic music as he has never been able to before.

In addition to shaping tones, glissandi, vibrati, and sequencing effects can be drawn upon. The beauty of a string-synthesizer combination is that the performer can use his experience and intuition of the string sound envelope and stringed instruments' continuity of frequency with (or in opposition to) the discrete (or discontinuous) frequency band of the keyboard.

E. <u>The power amplifier</u>: The power amplifier is the device that takes the voltage signal generated by the preamplifiers and effects devices and converts it into power that can drive a speaker system. Ultimately it produces high current with voltage fluctuation proportional to the incoming signal.

F. <u>The speaker system:</u> The speaker system, which is driven by the power amplifier is the device that converts electrical energy into mechanical energy. This mechanical energy sets the air in vibratory motion, thus creating that phenomenon we know as sound. Since the speaker system is also a transducer, it is one of the most critical components in a sound system.

G. <u>The power supply</u>: The power supply is the heart of any electronic system. It is the device that provides the working voltage to the various amplifiers and preamplifiers in the systems that are necessary for operation. The quality of the power supply can determine the quality of the amplifier and will be explained in another section of this chapter.

A RATIONAL METHOD FOR SELECTING AMPLIFIERS AND SPEAKER SYSTEMS

The selection of an amplifier and speaker combination for musical instrument amplification involves some complex problems, decisions, and evaluations. One cannot merely use the same guidelines for selecting a high fidelity or stereo system, yet one cannot entirely ignore them. In instrument amplification, especially for bass, one must consider very carefully his power requirements.

When one selects his amplifier and speaker system he generally can obtain a "spec" sheet on the amplifier and at least a power rating on the speaker. It is as much the buyer's responsibility to be able to read the specifications intelligently as it is the manufacturer's responsibility to print them honestly. The buyer can also learn how to judge the honesty of a manufacturer in relation to his power and distortion ratings. At present, power ratings of amplifiers are rather ambiguous. There are three forms of power ratings — all legitimate. The trick is to know how the rating is done and why it is significant. Power, $\underline{P}$ is expressed by the relationship $\underline{P} = EI$, where E =voltage and $\underline{I}$ =current. Power is the rate work is done or, in other terms, the rate energy is dissipated. Power may also be defined in terms of voltage across a resistive load or current through a resistive load. Using Ohm's law, $E = IR$, where $\underline{R}$ is the resistive load (in our case $\underline{R}$ simulates the speaker's impedance), we obtain the following power relationships:

$$\underline{P} = \underline{E}^2/\underline{R} \qquad\qquad \text{and} \qquad\qquad \underline{P} = I^2\,\underline{R}$$

These relationships are fine for direct current measurements, but music requires alternating current and alternating voltage analysis in order to accurately interpret power relationships in an amplifier.

There are currently three basic power rating systems for amplifier systems:

> A. RMS power, or continuous sine wave power
>
> B. IHF (Institute of High Fidelity) power, or music power
>
> C. Peak IHF power, or peak music power

The important thing for the musician to know is how to use the numbers that the manufacturer states in his specifications. It is immediately important to know that peak IHF power equals twice IHF power. But now comes the significant part: a reputable manufacturer will generally state both the RMS power and the IHF power. If they are roughly from 10 to 30

---

[2] The FRAP, incidentally, has a frequency response of 5 to 100,000 Hz, thus enabling the subharmonic structure of the tone to be amplified. Subharmonics are important as they reinforce the fundamentals just as harmonics do. They follow the sequence fo/2, fo/3, etc., where fo is the fundamental and fo/2 is the first subharmonic, fo/3 the record, etc.

percent within each other's value (the IHF power will always be higher) then the amplifier should be considered quite stable and fairly low in distortion.[3] The reputable manufacturer should also publish distortion figures along with his power figures.[4] The two should go hand in hand. If there is an extreme difference between the RMS and the IHF power, a poor amplifier is indicated because of inadequate power supply regulation.

For example: A manufacturer gives the peak IHF power or peak music power as 160 watts and the RMS power as 55 watts. Divide the peak power of 160 watts by 2 to obtain IHF power. This is 80 watts. Next divide 80 into 55 and multiply by 100. Subtract this figure from 100 to obtain the difference percentage which in this case is 31. The amplifier is acceptable.

One of the most important features of any power amplifier is the quality of its power supply, in terms of both filtering and regulation. It is also the section of an amplifier which generally causes the most breakdown problems, so it is always a good thing to inquire about the power supply quality (the salesman may even treat you with more respect if he thinks that you are knowledgeable). You see, in many amplifiers, as the power goes up the voltages to the amplifying section of the amplifier drop (especially in sustained notes) and thus the frequency response suffers and distortion occurs. This is due to poor power supply regulation. If the amplifier has a well-regulated, well-filtered power supply, you can reasonably assume that it is also quite reliable. Reliability is probably the most important feature that a musician must search for in an amplifier. Thus, by careful examination of amplifier specs, a great deal can be assumed about the design characteristics.

The next specification, and one no less important than the others mentioned, is the impedance match of the speakers to the amplifier. This is critical because unless the impedance is matched properly, some tones will be louder than others and the system will lose power. Electronically stated: maximum power transfer occurs when the output of one system (in this case the amplifier) equals the input or load impedance of the system the power is being fed to, which is in our case the speaker system. If impedance doesn't match, then power is dissipated in the form of heat rather than sound. Remember the adage: "As the impedance grows, the power goes." This is even more critical for transistor amplifiers than tube amplifiers. If the tap on the amplifier calls for a speaker system of four ohms, then the total impedance of your speaker system should total four ohms. Virtually all

---

[3] Howard M. Tremain, The Audio Cyclopedia (Sams Publications, 1969), p. 1556.

[4] It should be noted that in the case of stereo amplifiers, the power figure is traditionally the sum of the channels. Each channel must be considered separately, so divide the power given by 2 unless the figure is given as watts per channel.

speaker systems that are "off the shell" will give the impedance of the speaker system. For
the do-it-yourselfer, the problem is more difficult.. He must consider both groups of
speakers and, in the case of woofers (low frequency speakers), midrange speakers, and
tweeter (high frequency speakers) combinations, frequency dividing networks as
well. The frequency dividing network, or crossover, insures that the correct frequency
group goes to the right speaker. This is also a protective device — in the case of a tweeter,
or some midrange speakers, the low tones, unless shunted away, will ruin the tweeter.

The amount of sound power a speaker can produce is proportional to the area of its cone.
The name of the game is moving air. Low tones are much more difficult to reproduce because it is difficult to set large amounts of air in vibration at low frequencies. So select
the largest speaker or set of speakers that you can afford or need.

In the case of a packaged system (amplifier and speaker in one cabinet) it can only be
assumed that the speaker-amplifier power relationship is OK and the speaker impedance
matches the amplifier's.

Now that the speaker system is selected, the last step is the enclosure or cabinet that
will house your speaker system. Please, please don't pick this point to decide to skimp.
The importance of a well-designed and well-built enclosure cannot be stressed enough. A
fine speaker in a poor cabinet is almost always worse sounding than a mediocre speaker in
a really well designed enclosure. The two should be considered as one. When you finally
select a system you must listen to the speaker of your choice in a matching cabinet. This,
after the electrical requirements are fulfilled and the size of the speaker system deter-
mined, is the only way to select a speaker system. It is from this point on a matter of
personal taste because all speakers, just as basses, have a characteristic sound. In the
case of high power and low frequency response it is recommended that one use a large,
well-designed, hermetically sealed and insulated enclosure. The wood should not be less
than 3/4-inch plywood and each panel braced to limit cabinet vibrations. Glue and screws
should be used in its construction. The enclosure should be hermetically sealed to provide
a cushion of air as the speaker goes in its backward excursion and a damping as it goes in
its forward excursion. Like all vibrating objects, speakers producing low notes move
slower but move further. Therefore, a speaker used to produce low notes will soon tear
itself apart because of its violent backward and forward vibration if it is not constrained by
a sealed cabinet. This is an effect produced by continuous high power but it must still be
taken into consideration. So if you are going into high power for bass amplification, don't
forget the speaker cabinet. It should be large enough to house the speaker and sealed
enough to provide a cushion of air. If a sealed cabinet is used, the amplifier should not be
in the sealed portion of the cabinet as this will prevent the amplifier from dissipating its
heat. All amplifiers produce heat that must be dissipated for proper operation.

This should provide some guidelines for optimizing the selection of an amplifier speaker system. For those who want to explore further I recommend the book by Alexander Schure and Jack Darr listed in the bibliography to this chapter.

We still haven't decided on criteria regarding how much power an amplifier should have. Although I cannot give off-the-cuff figures, I can give some guide to approaching the problem. You should consider the different environments that you will encounter — whether the room will be large or small, heavily draped or furnitured, live or dead. Then and only then should you examine the various amplifiers on the market and choose the one that will do your biggest job in terms of power. When you have decided on a power figure (it does not really matter whether it is RMS or IHF power as long as you are consistent) then you should start poring over the specifications in the manner I have just described. I realize that many manufacturers do not publish all the pertinent information, partly because of their opinion that musicians don't need such complications, but maybe enough inquiries will bring this about. You as bass players should be most concerned because clean, undistorted bass notes are the hardest tones to reproduce.

I will not discuss tone controls or effects devices because these things a person should decide for himself. The prospective amplifier buyer should always be sure that it is well fused and has a polarity switch to minimize hum.

After choosing an amplifier the next thing you must do is find a set of speakers and cabinets that match it.

The choosing of a speaker system is a matter of personal taste governed by a few basic rules and considerations. First, a speaker should be chosen that can take the power that you are going to pour into it. This should be the continuous sine wave or RMS power. It goes without saying that the speaker should be able to reproduce the lowest tone of the bass, which is about 40 Hz in the case of the E string. I would shoot for 20 or 30 Hz just to cover everything. It is absolutely essential to get a speaker or set of speakers that can handle your power or you will run first into distortion and then into a blown speaker. You see, if the speaker can't handle the power, the voice coil heats up and distorts its shape. Since it must move back and forth in a very close tolerance assembly, it will then rub and not move smoothly, thus distorting the tone. If it distorts and then gets hung up in one spot, the heat or power will dissipate in the voice coil and not in the form of mechanical motion. The voice coil will just burn out. This is why it cannot be stressed enough how important it is to find a speaker system that can handle your power requirements.[5]

---

[5] For those interested in delving far into the terms relating to speakers, there is a very fine set of articles in the November 1969, December 1969, and January 1970 issues of Audio Magazine entitled, "Layman's Guide to Loudspeaker Specifications," by Victor Brociner.

USING THE POWER AT HAND

You have selected a system that you really believe in. Now you have the responsibility to use it to fullest advantage. This is where the real work begins. Just as you have developed your technique, you will have to put in the same kind of effort using your electronics to gain fine technique. I suggest first learning to hear your instrument. There is a very good chance that you do not know what your instrument sounds like to a listener. Get a friend to play your bass and stand right in front of it. Listen! Start moving away from your instrument and listen how the sound quality changes. Then do the same thing but at angles from the front of the bass. You will again hear a change of sound quality and volume. This is because instruments have sound distribution patterns. You play the bass from behind and you do not get to hear what it sounds like to an audience. Once you have an idea of how it sounds, then you can develop a sense of what you desire. Place your pickup (if you are using a FRAP) in various areas of the instrument and listen for the type of sound you want to obtain. If you are using a mike, do the same thing by moving the mike. If you are using a magnetic or a fixed position piezoelectric pickup, then you can only use tone controls or filters to change your sound quality. After finding placement that you like, adjust your tone controls to suit your taste.

Then learn to use volume. When using electronic amplification, you will not have to bow as hard or pluck as hard to be heard. A new control of facilities must be gained. There must be developed a feeling of solidarity and fullness as opposed to sheer volume. Intensity must be without overwork. You are amplified, a turn of the volume control will give power, but at the same time you must learn to play pianissimo with the same system and still have a solid tone. This should have been developed before getting amplified, but now it must be done even more critically. As you have gotten a feeling of how your bass sounds, you should also get a feeling of how your speaker sounds. Do the same exercise with your speakers that you have done with your bass. They also will have a distribution pattern. You should also do this when selecting a speaker system. Some speaker systems are great for small halls but will sound thin in a large auditorium.

Get a feeling for how long a tone will sustain when amplified. You will undoubtedly find that your criteria for tone fadeout will change. The amplification system will bring out tones that would have been considered delayed before the amplifier was used. Learn to use this extra sound duration.

FEEDBACK

Feedback is an annoyance that has plagued the musician since the advent of microphones. Everyone who uses amplifiers has had some problem, at one time or another, with feedback. As the power goes up so does the feedback potential. With a thorough understanding of the causes it can be reduced, eliminated, or controlled so we can use it musically.

Feedback occurs when the sound produced by the speakers causes the instrument or the strings (or both) to vibrate sympathetically. The microphone or pickup picks up the sympathetic vibrations and amplifies them. The speaker goes through the same procedure again and again, building up a resonance and in a fraction of a second's time we have the infamous howl known as feedback. Microphones are the worst offenders because they can do it without even being near an instrument (the microphone becomes the instrument).

The answer to controlling feedback lies in geometric placement of the instrument in relation to the speakers. Stay as far away from the speakers as possible and experiment with angular placement as well. If the instrument is placed in such a way that the phase angle of the instrument's vibrations is 180 degrees out of phase with the speakers', then it will be very difficult to cause feedback. This can be demonstrated by causing feedback with your instrument and reducing it by turning the instrument in any direction. By doing this we can begin to set the feeling of control. Conversely, if at a climactic moment the performer turns toward the amplifier, feedback can be produced.

It should be noted that some amplifiers are more conducive to feedback than others because of a circuitry design that can send them into resonance easily. This information can be obtained from knowledgeable and reliable dealers.

VOLTS, AMPERES, OHMS, WATTS, AND DECIBELS

Almost everyone has at one time or another heard the terms volts, amperes, ohms, watts, and decibels, but few people actually know what they mean. These are all words that are used, with the exception of decibels, in everyday conversation. When a fuse blows at home we replace it with a new one of perhaps 20 amperes. Our electric bill gets higher if we leave lamps of 150 and 200 watts on needlessly. We go into a store and ask for a flashlight battery of maybe 1 1/2 volts. A heating wire may have a resistance of 30 ohms. What does all this mean and how does this apply to audio electronics?

Volts. The volt is a unit of potential rise. It is expressed in terms of energy per electrical charge. For example, in a 1 1/2 volt battery, the plus terminal has a rise if 1 1/2 volts in relation to the minus terminal. The minus terminal is therefore 1 1/2 volts below the plus terminal. Voltage is only significant when it is related to something else. It is a unit of electromotive force and a measure of the energy it takes to move an electron from one place to another. When we speak of a peak to peak voltage of 10 to 1,000 Hz, we mean that in the time of one second there is a voltage rise of five volts then a voltage drop of five volts occurring 1,000 times. The rise from minus 5 to plus 5 is, of course, 10. Thus the peak to peak voltage is 10. In audio we encounter voltages on tube elements, transistor elements, and other circuit components. When voltage is too high for some parts it can sometimes destroy them by arcing through insulation or burning contacts. We also talk about how much voltage a device can take without distorting or how much voltage an amplifier needs (input voltage) to drive it to full output.

Amperes.   Amperes relate to current flow, analogous to water flow. They are expressed in terms of coulombs (electrical charge) per second. In wire circuits, the flow of charge is mainly that of the negative charge carried by electrons; thus the positive direction of current flow is opposite to the actual direction of electron flow. A point not commonly stressed is that the electrons in a conductor actually move quite slowly — it is the fact of conduction which travels at the speed of light. Analogously, water may flow slowly through a pipe, yet when the water is turned on at one end of a filled pipe it comes out almost immediately, the delay depending on the speed of a pressure wave in water. Electrical current is usually drawn from one device to another. For example, a speaker will draw current from the power amplifier. The current drawn into the speaker will operate the speaker and the voltage that the current will have will determine how much power the speaker will put out.

Ohms.   The ohm is a unit of electrical resistance. It is expressed as volts per amperes (Ohm's Law). The ohm is a measure of impedance, and impedance is the slowing down of current. In audio, as well as in other branches of electronics, we are concerned with impedance matching and using impedance to limit current. We use impedance matching devices to preserve frequency response and signal or to alter signals. Impedance matching is very significant when transferring power from one device to another. Devices have both input and output impedance. An amplifier will generally have impedances of 4, 8, and 16 ohms for output impedance. Speakers come with either 4, 8, or 16 ohms for input. To get maximum performance, the impedance of the speakers must be matched with the impedance of the amplifier.

Watts.   The watt is a unit of power. It can be converted to joules per second or horsepower or any other unit of energy per time. Power is the rate of doing work or the rate of expending energy. We are concerned with energy per time when we talk of power. When we say an amplifier puts out sixty watts, we mean that it expends a quantity of energy per unit time. It is also expressed as volts times amperes. We consider power when we drive speakers because too much of it will destroy the speaker by transmitting too much heat in a unit time before the speaker can dissipate the heat. You see, electrical energy just like any other kind of energy can be converted to other kinds of energy.

Decibels.   Decibel is, in my opinion, the most misused and misunderstood term in audio and electronics. The term refers to the intensity level of sound and is expressed as:

$$dB = 10 \log(\underline{1}/\underline{1}_o)$$

where $\underline{1}$ is the intensity of sound and $\underline{1}_o$ is the threshold intensity. $\underline{1}$ is generally expressed as watts per square meter. The threshold intensity is the threshold of hearing in watts per square meter. As we see, this is a logarithm of a power ratio. We can then relate it to power ratios of electronic quantities if we define a $\underline{P}_o$ (power level to relate everything to). A dB is generally defined as 1 milliwatt into a load of 600 ohms. Thus for a power gain or increase dB is expressed as:

$$\underline{dB} = 10 \log (\underline{P}_2/\underline{P}_1)$$

where $\underline{P}_1$ equals the power in and $\underline{P}_2$ equals the power out. We can also use dB to express voltage or current gain, but a different formula is used and the input and output impedances of the circuits must be specified unless they are equal.

BASIC BIBLIOGRAPHY

For those who wish to delve further into the world of electronics or are baffled by the many terms relating to audio or electronics, a basic list of references is provided below:

Allied Radio Corporation. Dictionary of Electronic Terms, Chicago: Allied Radio Corporation.

Backus, John, The Acoustical Foundations of Music, New York: W. W. Norton, 1969.

Darr, Jack, Electric Guitar Amplifier Handbook, Sams Publications, 1969.

Langford-Smith, F. Radiotron Designer's Handbook, Harrison, N.J.: RCA Electronic Components, 1953.

Music Educator's Journal, "Glossary of Electronic Terms," Music Educator's Journal 55 (November, 1968).

RCA Transistor Manual.

RCA Tube Manual.

Schure, Alexander, Impedance Matching, Rider Publications, 1963.

Strange, Allen, Electronic Music — Systems, Techniques and Controls, Iowa: Wm. C. Brown, 1971.

Tremaine, Howard M. The Audio Cyclopedia, Sams Publications, 1969.

Walsh, J.B., and Miller, K.S. Introductory Electric Circuits, New York: McGraw-Hill, 1960.

Winckel, Fritz, Music, Sound and Sensation, New York: Dover Press, 1967.

Appendix

Kingdom of Italy
Ministry of the National Economy
Bureau of Intellectual Property

Industrial Patent No. 243592, Luigi Russolo, Milan, Italy.
Musical Instrument of variable Stringlength with Damped Activation.
Category X; A (nno) IV (1926)

Issued December 11, 1925
Active from Oct. 24, 1925

In all previously known string instruments, the strings are set in motion by means of single or repeated percussion or plucking, or else by means of stroking with a rugged, flexible device. In certain instruments is to be found a multiplicity of strings of a fixed, invariable length; in other words, the string length may be varied by means of transversal pressure against a fingerboard.

The object of the present invention is a musical instrument of variable string length, characterized by the fact that the activation of the string, and the determination of its length, are accomplished by means of the same device, capable of immobilizing the string immediately after causing its vibration, in the same, or in any other point along the string in which vibration had been caused, in such manner as to bring about the simultaneous and independent vibration of two segments of the same string, thus producing a bitonal combination of two complementary sounds. It is further characterized by providing the activating mechanism with variable dampers, so that the oscillation of one of the vibrating segments may be reduced at will, in such a way as to permit gradual reduction of the bichord to a single note. Finally, it is equipped with a device capable of rapid reiteration of both activation and damping of the strings, by which intensification and prolongation of sounds is achieved.

Manners of adaptation of the present invention may vary according to the nature of the instrument to which it is to be adapted; harps, mandolins, viols. In the present exposition, only instruments belonging to the latter family are to be considered (i. e., violins, violas, violoncellos, and contrabasses), but it must also be understood that these single considerations and realizations may be extended, by obvious modification, to include instruments of the other families, such as, for example, mandolins, etc.

The allied drawing represents, for schematic and demonstrative purposes, the execution of a practical model as seen in two separate views (horizontal, vertical).

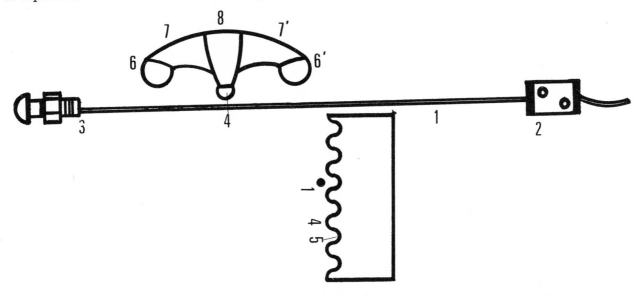

In the case of the application hereby illustrated, it is supposed that there is a single string (1), threaded from a clamp (2), and attached at (3) to any mechanism designed to regulate its tension, such as an ordinary screw, as in above drawing. The instrument may, of course, employ several strings, and may furthermore be furnished with a sounding-board, one or more bridges of appropriate height, etc. The activating mechanism determining string length must be, above all, so constituted as to move the string from its resting position to set it into vibration, and subsequently stop it at the point in which it had been activated. Thus, for example, a hammer or a plectrum, after percussion or plucking of the string, may return to rest in contact with it; a bow may provide, after a convex or raised scraping surface (4), a cavity (5), so that the string thereby activated is held in place and stopped by the cavity itself in such manner as to produce a node in the corresponding point of the string length. In order to intensify the sound and render it continuous, this bow may have a succession of concave and convex surfaces, being teethed, screw-shaped, or containing similar "threading."

With this device, if the string is activated at variable points between the fret and the mid-point, one obtains from the longer segment all the pitches included between the fundamental and the octave, which may be taken from any scale as desired: equal-tempered, diatonic, semichromatic, enharmonic, or others, as well as all the intermediate pitches. At the same time, the other segment of the string yields complementary pitches; thus, for example, if positions resulting in a normal diatonic scale are used, the following series of bichords is obtained, supposing the fundamental to be (c_1):

$$(c_1\text{-}0); \quad (d_1\text{-}d_4); \quad (e_1\text{-}e_3); \quad (f_1\text{-}c_3);$$
$$(g_1\text{-}g_2); \quad (a_1\text{-}e_2); \quad (b_1\text{-}c_2 \natural); \quad (c_2\text{-}c_2).$$

In continuing the motion of the bow towards the bridge or the fret the others, inverse, combinations of the above series will be obtained. It is to be noted that all the above-mentioned bichords are consonant at the unison, octave, and the fifth, with the exception of one containing a large second. However, it is not the present undertaking to present a musical theory of the above-mentioned instrument, nor for this practical model, nor for the other model mentioned, nor for still other possible ones not described herein.

It is obvious that an instrument thus constructed is able to produce extremely variable and unusual timbric qualities; it is furthermore capable of producing single sounds instead of bichords; this may be accomplished simply through provision of a means by which to dampen either one or the other segment of the string.

In the practical model described, the activating bow is equipped with two lateral dampers (6, 6') of smooth material, held in place by supports (7, 7') joined to the body of the bow (8); by tipping the bow to the left or right along its longitudinal plane, the vibration of that portion of the string which is either to the left or to the right of the point of damped activation is impeded. Normally one damper would prove sufficient; the presence of two dampers may be useful in simplifying the performance of large interval jumps, or in order to shorten the distance the bow must travel along a segment of the string. The first octave, for example, may be played while damping the segment nearer the fret (or bridge), and the other octaves by the reverse of this procedure, while damping the segment nearer the bridge (or fret). One may of course mark the desired notes and combinations of notes with appropriate signs along a fingerboard.

The details of construction may vary according to the nature of the instrument desired, without its falling outside the realm of this invention.

VINDICATIONS

1. Musical instrument of variable string length, characterized by the fact that the activation of the string and the determination of its length are accomplished by means of the same device, capable of immobilizing the string immediately after causing its vibration, in the same, or in any other point along the string in which vibration had been caused, in such manner as to bring about the simultaneous and independent vibration of two segments of the same string, thus producing a bitonal combination of two sounds.

2. Musical instrument as in (1), further characterized by providing the activating mechanism with variable dampers, so that the oscillation of one of the vibrating segments may be reduced at will, in such a way as to permit gradual reduction of the bichord to a single note.

3. Musical instrument as in (1) and (2), equipped with a device capable of rapid reiteration of both activation and damping of the strings, by which intensification and prolongation of sounds is achieved.

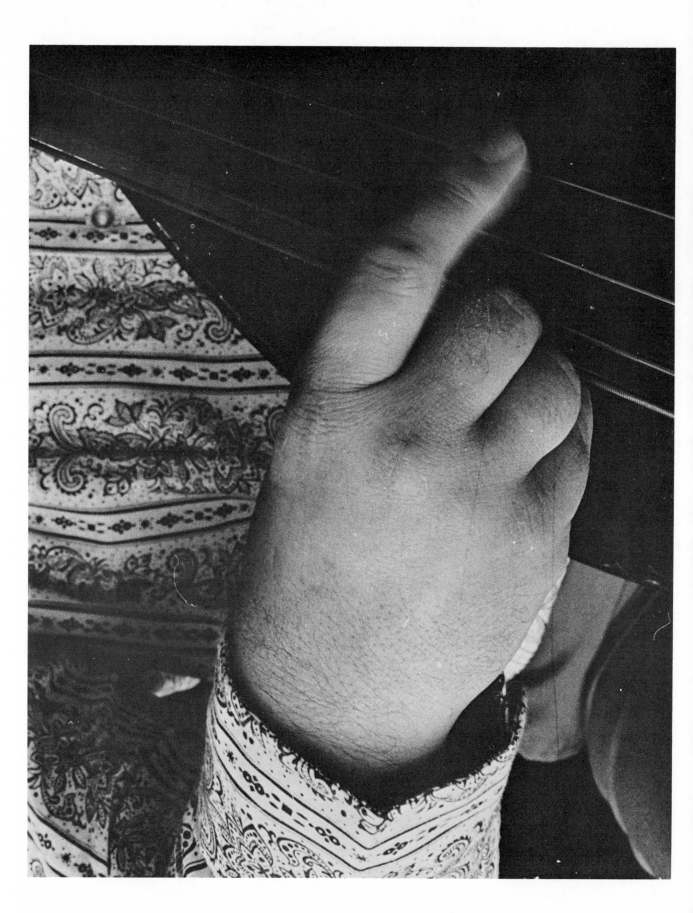

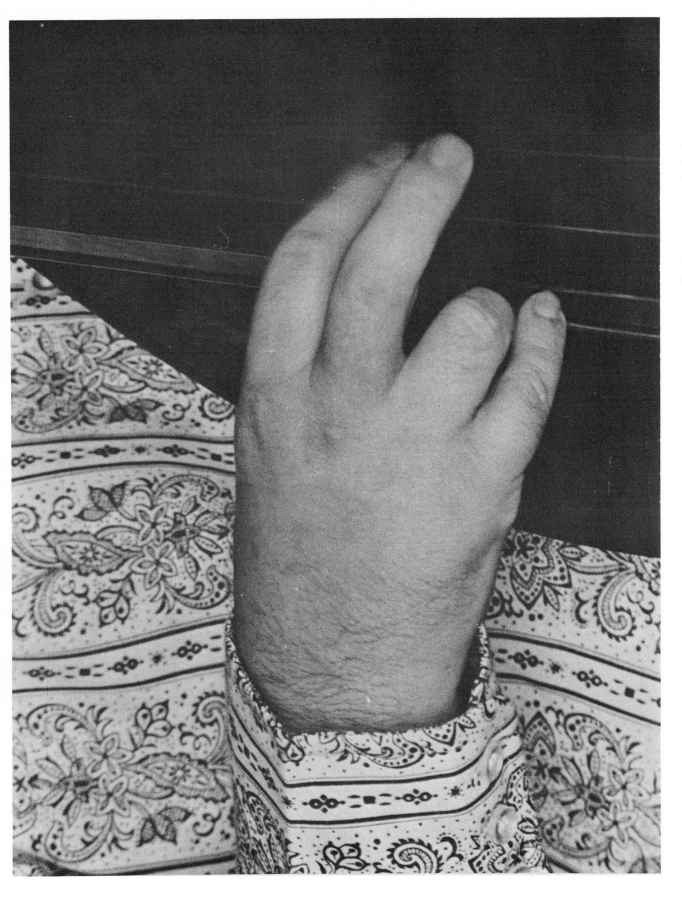

2. Pizzacato tremolo (2 fingers)

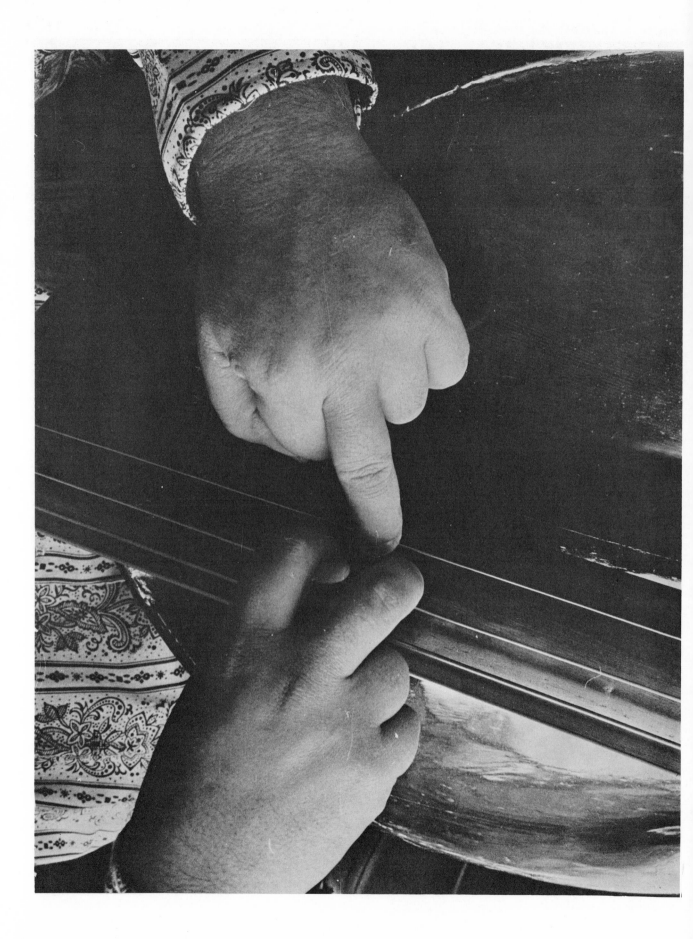

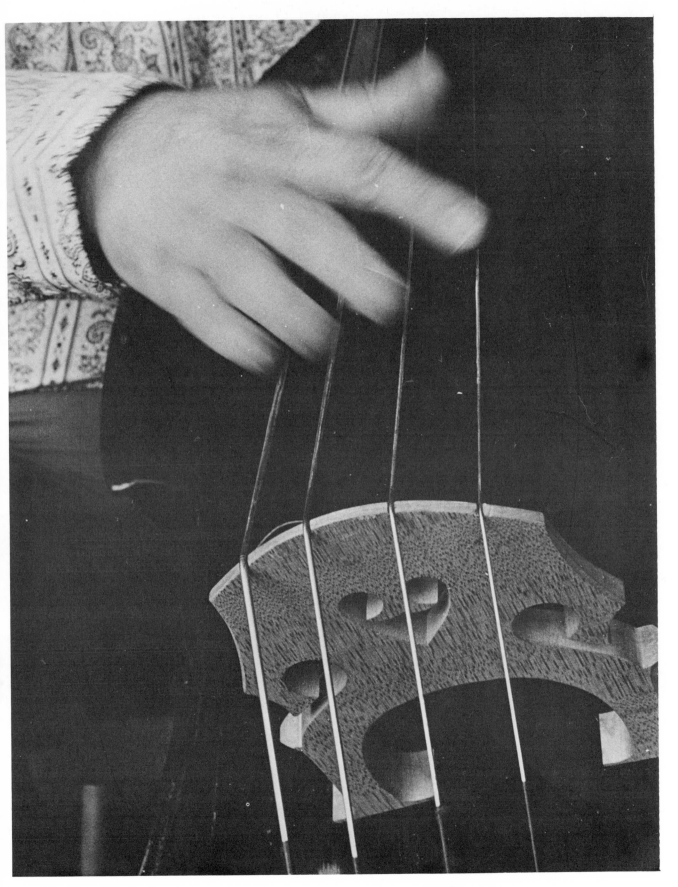

4. "Drumming"

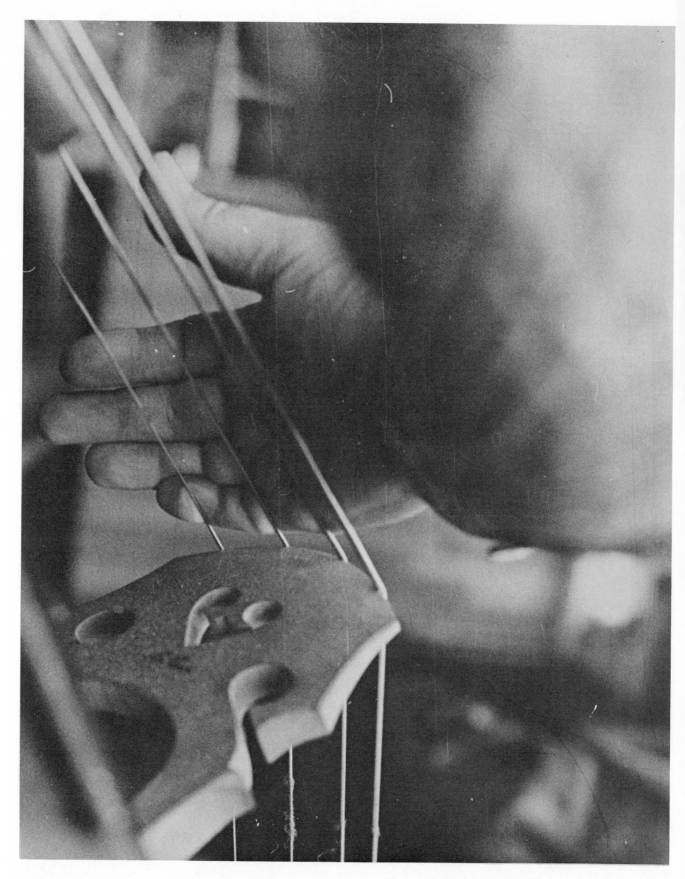

5. Pizzicato muta

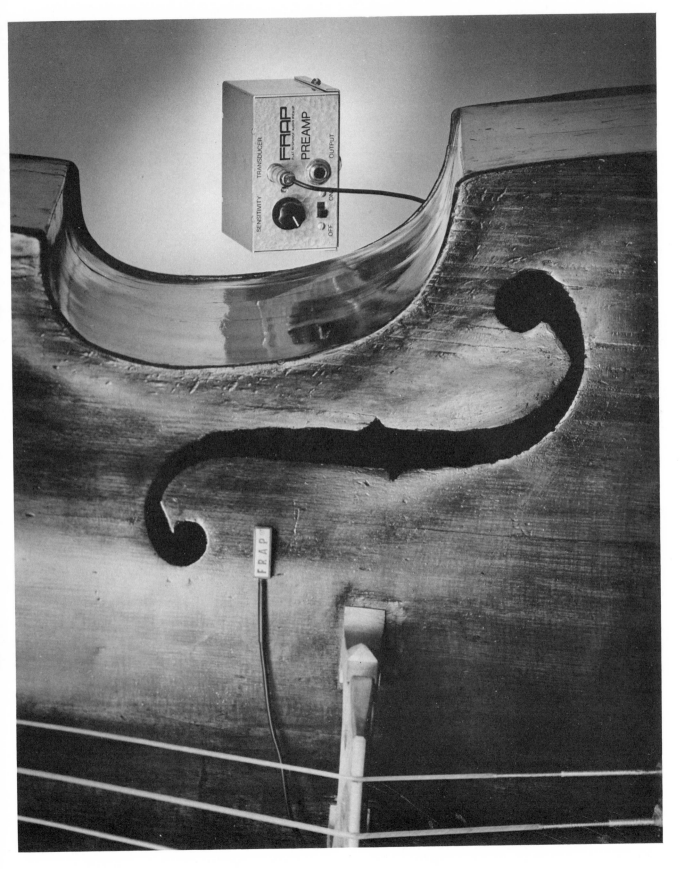

6. Frap transducer

Bibliography

Music

Austin, Larry. Bass: A theater piece in open style for string bass, player, tape and film (1966). Composer, Performer Edition, Tampa, Florida.

Biber, Heinrich. Battalia for Strings and Continuo. Broude Brothers, N.Y., N.Y.

Bille, Isaiah. Scherzo, Organum. Ricordi c/o Franco Columbo Music, N.Y., N.Y.

Bottesini, Giovanni. Concerto No. 2 in B. Minor. McGinnis and Marx Music, N.Y., N.Y.

Burt, George. Exit Music for 12 Players (1968). Composer c/o School of Music, University of Michigan, Ann Arbor, Michigan.

Cage, John. Solo for Bass (1957-1958). 26'1. 1499" For a String Player (1955). C. F. Peters Corporation, N.Y., N.Y.

Chihara, Paul. Logs (1969). C. F. Peters Corp., N.Y., N.Y.

Childs, Barney. Mr. T., His Fancy (1967). American Composers Alliance, N.Y., N.Y.
Sonata for Bass Alone (1960). McGinnis and Marx, N.Y., N.Y.
Jack's New Bag (1966). Composer, Performer Edition.

Cope, David. Cycles (1969).
Alternatives (1968). Composers Autograph Publications, Cleveland, Ohio.

Crumb, George. Three Madrigals for Soprano, Vibraphone and Contrabass (1965). Mill's Music, N.Y., N.Y.
Songs, Drones and Refrains of Death (1969). Composer c/o Music Dept. University of Pennsylvania, Philadelphia, Pennsylvania 19104.

Curran, Alvin. Homemade (1968). Composer, Performer Edition. Tampa, Florida.

Deak, Jon. Color Studies for Contrabass (1969).
Surrealist Studies (1970). Media Press, Champaign-Urbana, Illinois.

Diemente, Edward. Unvelopment (1968). SeeSaw Music Corporation, N.Y., N.Y.

Dittersdorf, Carl Ditters von. Concerto for Contrabass in Eb Major. B. Schott's Sonne, Mainz und Leipzig.

Dragonetti, Domenico. Concerto for Contrabasse. Bote und Bock, Berlin, Germany.

BIBLIOGRAPHY

Druckman, Jacob. <u>Valentine</u> (1969). MCA Music, N.Y., N.Y.

Erb, Donald. <u>VII Miscellaneous</u> (1964).
    <u>Reconnaissance</u> (1967).
    <u>In No Strange Land</u> (1968).
    <u>Trio for Two</u> (1968).
    <u>Basspiece</u> (1969). Theodore Presser Company, Bryn Mawr, Pennsylvania.

Erickson, Robert. <u>Ricercar á 3</u> (1967). University of California Press, Los Angeles, California.

Felciano, Richard. <u>Spectra</u> (1966). E. C. Schirmer, Boston, Mass.

Fisher, Stephen. <u>Concertpiece</u> (1962-1968). C. F. Peters Corp., N.Y., N.Y.

Frederickson, Thomas. <u>Music for the Double Bass Alone</u> (1963).
    <u>Music for Five Instruments</u> (1965). Theodore Presser Company.

Gaburo, Kenneth. <u>Two</u> (1963). Theodore Presser Company.
    <u>Antiphony IV</u> (1966-1967).
    <u>Inside</u> (1969). c/o Composer, Music Dept., University of California at San Diego, La Jolla, California 92037.

Harrison, Lou. <u>Suite for Symphonic Strings</u> (1960-1963). C. F. Peters, N.Y., N.Y.

Hodkinson, Sydney. <u>Interplay</u> (1966). Composer c/o School of Music, University of Michigan, Ann Arbor, Michigan.

Hoffman, Allen. <u>Recitative and Aria for Solo Contrabass</u> (1964). Composer c/o Hartt College of Music, University of Hartford, West Hartford, Conn.

Kagel, Mauricio. <u>Sonant</u> (1960-). C. F. Peters, N.Y., N.Y.

Kupferman, Meyer. <u>Infinities 24</u> (1968). General Music, N.Y., N.Y.

Kurtz, Eugene. <u>Improvisations for Contrabass</u> (1968). Edition Jobert, Paris.

Lanza, Alcides. <u>Strobo</u> (1968). Boosey and Hawkes, N.Y., N.Y.

McCarty, Frank. <u>Bert Bells, Bows, Balls the Bass</u> (1970). Media Press, Champaign-Urbana, Illinois.

Mizelle, John. <u>Degree of Change</u> (1967). Composer, Performer Edition. Tampa, Florida.

Monteverdi, Claudio. <u>Ill Combattimento di Tancredi e Clorinda</u> (1627). Broude Brothers, N.Y., N.Y.

Moryl, Richard. <u>Systems</u> (1968). General Music, N.Y., N.Y.

Moss, Lawrence. <u>Windows</u> (1966). SeeSaw Music, N.Y., N.Y.

Oliveros, Pauline. <u>Doublebasses at Twenty Paces</u> (1968). Composer c/o Music Dept., University of California at San Diego, La Jolla, California 92037.

Peck, Russell. <u>I db</u> (1968). Composer c/o Professor B. Turetzky, Music Dept., University of California at San Diego, La Jolla, California 92037

Penderecki, C. Threnody to the Victims of Hiroshima (1961).
                Capriccio for Oboe and Strings (1965).
                Polymorphia (1961). PWN Edition, Moeck Verlag Celle.

Perle, George. Monody No. 2 for Solo Double Bass (1962). Theodore Presser Company.

Peterson, Wayne. Phantasmagoria (1968). SeeSaw Music, N. Y., N. Y.

Phillips, Peter. Sonata for String Bass (1964). McGinnis and Marx, N. Y., N. Y.
                  Divertimento for Three String Basses (1968). Murbo Music, N. Y., N. Y.

Rabe, Folke. Pajazzo (1963). Composer c/o Rikskonserter, Box 5070, 10242 Stockholm
              5, Sweden.

Reck, David. Night Sounds (and Dream) (1965). Composer, Performer Edition.

Richmond, Kim. Trio (1961). Composer c/o American Federation of Musicians, Local
                47, Los Angeles, California.

Schwartz, Elliot. Dialogue for Solo Contrabass (1966). Carl Fischer, N. Y., N. Y.

Sender, Ramon. Balances (1970). c/o Professor B. Turetzky, Music Dept., University
                of California at San Diego, La Jolla, California 92037.

Shapey, Ralph. De Profundis (1960). Composer c/o Music Dept., University of Chicago,
                Chicago, Illinois.

Swift, Richard. Thrones (1966). American Composers Alliance. N. Y., N. Y.

Sydeman, William. For Double Bass Alone (1959). McGinnis and Marx, N. Y., N. Y.
                   Duo for Trumpet and Doublebass (1969). SeeSaw Music, N. Y., N. Y.

Von Biel, Michael. String Quartet II (1963). Universal Edition.

Von Wrochem. Limelight (1968). Composers Autograph Publications, Cleveland, Ohio.

Whittenberg, Charles. Conversations for Double Bass Solo (1968). C. F. Peters, N. Y.,
                       N. Y.

Wilson, Olly. Piece for Four (1966). Composer c/o Music Dept., University of
               California, Berkeley, California.

Wuorinen, Charles. Turetzky Pieces (1960). McGinnis and Marx, N. Y., N. Y.
                    Concerto for Double Bass Alone)1961). American Composer's
          Alliance. N. Y., N. Y.

Yuasa, Jogi. Triplicity for Contrabass (1970). Ongaku-No-Tomo Sha Corp., Tokyo, Japan.

Articles

Drager, Hans-Heinz. "Kontrabass." Die Musik in Geschichte und Gegenwart 7: 1518-1522.

Gelinck, M. "On the Bow of the Double-Bass." The Harmonicon 7 (December 1829): 298.

_____. "Remarks on the Double-Bass." The Harmonicon 7 (December 1829):
          297-298.

Huber, Ernest. "History of the Double Bass." Pacific Coast Musician 207 (1962): 78-84.

_____. "Der Kontrabass." Mitteilungsblatt des Kontrabassisten Bundes. Leipzig: Nos. 1-5 (Mar. 1929, Feb. 1931).

Metcalfe, Allen. "Solo-Music for the Double Bass." The Strad 70 (1959): 55-57.

Piper, Towry. "Concerning Double Basses." The Strad 21, 22 (Feb. -June 1911): 358-359, 393-394, 431-432, 19-21, 55-56.

Planyavsky, Alfred. "Der Kontrabass in der Kammermusik," Osterreichiche Musik-zeitschrift 13 (1958): 57-63.

Sanky, Stuart. "On the Notation of Harmonics for the Double Bass." Bulletin of the American Composers Alliance 6 (Autumn 1956): 9-10.

Sklar, Philip. "Concerning the Contrabass." The Etude 66 (1948): 477-509.

Turetzky, Bertram. "Notes on the Bass." Source 1 (1967): 1.

_____. "The Bass as a Drum." The Bass Sound Post 1 (1969).

_____. "Vocal and Speech Sounds — A Technique of Contemporary Writing for the Contrabass." The Composer 1 (1969).

Verkoeyen, Jos. "String Players and New Music." Sonorum Speculum 45 (Winter 1970): 18-26.

Books

Andersen, Arthur Olaf. Practical Orchestration. Boston: C. C. Birchard & Co., 1929.

Becker, Heinz. History of Instrumentation, trans. K. G. Fellerer. Cologne: Arn Volk Verlag, 1964.

Berlioz-Strauss. Treatise on Instrumentation. New York: Kalmus, 1903.

Bottesini, Giovanni. Complete Method for the Contre-Basse, trans. F. Clayton. London: Riviere et Hawkes, 1870.

Carse, Adam. The History of Orchestration. London: Kegan, Paul, Trench, Trubner and Co., Ltd., J. Curwen and Sons, Ltd., 1925.

_____. The Orchestra in the XVIIIth Century. Cambridge: W. Heffner and Sons Ltd., 1940.

_____. The Orchestra from Beethoven to Berlioz. New York: Broude Brothers, 1949.

Cohen, Irving. "The Historical Development of the Bouble Bass." Ph.D. dissertation, New York University, 1967.

Coon, Oscar. Harmony and Instrumentation. Cincinnati, Ohio: A. Squire, 1883.

Cruft, Eugene. The Eugene Cruft School of Double Bass Playing. London: Oxford University Press, 1966.

Elgar, Raymond. _Introduction to the Double Bass_. Sussex: Published by the author, 1960.

_____. _More About the Double Bass_. Sussex: Published by the author, 1963.

_____. _Looking at the Double Bass_. Sussex: Published by the author, 1967.

Forsyth, Cecil. _Orchestration_. New York: The MacMillan Company, 1947.

Friedheim, John. _Instructions for Playing the Double or Contra Bass_. Boston: Oliver Ditson and Co., 1870.

Gevaert, Francois Auguste. _Nouveau Traite General d'instrumentation_. Paris: Lemoine & Cie., 1885.

Hofmann, Richard. _Practical Instrumentation_. New York: G. Schirmer, 1893.

Jadassohn, Salomon. _Lehrbuch der Instrumentation_. Leipzig: Breitkopf und Hartel, 1889.

Kastner, Jean Georges. _Cours d'instrumentation_. Paris: Menstrel, Meissonier, Heugel, 1839.

Kennan, Kent Wheeler. _Technique of Orchestration_. New York: Prentice-Hall, 1952.

Kunitz, Hans. _Violoncello Kontrabass_. Die Instrumentation, vol. 13. Leipzig: Breitkopf und Hartel, 1961.

Piston, Walter. _Orchestration_. New York: W. W. Norton, 1955.

Prout, Ebenezer. _Instrumentation_. London: Novello and Company, 1877.

_____. _Technique of the Instruments_. The Orchestra, vol. 1 of 2. London: Augener Ltd., 1898.

Rauscher, Donald J. _Orchestration Scores and Scoring_. New York: The Free Press of Glencoe, 1963.

Read, Gardner. _Thesaurus of Orchestral Devices_, London. London: Sir Isaac Pitman and Sons, 1953.

Reicha, Anton. _Reicha's Orchestral Primer_. New York: Wm. Hall and Son, 1848.

Rimsky-Korsakow, Nicolas. _Principles of Orchestration_, ed. Maximilian Steinberg, trans. Edward Agate. Scarsdale, N.Y.: E. F. Kalmus, 1913.

Rogers, Bernard. _The Art of Orchestration_. New York: Appleton-Century-Crofts, 1951.

Simandl, Franz. _New Method for the Double Bass_. New York: Carl Fischer, 1904.

Sturm, Wilhelm. _Practische Contrabass—Schule_. Frankfurt am Main: Andre, 1877.

Warnecke, Friedrich. _Das Studium des Kontrabass—Spiels_. Hanover: Louis Oertel, 1909.

Wellesz, Egon. _Die Neue Instrumentation_. Berlin: M. Hesse, 1929.

White, A. C. _The Double Bass_, ed. F. A. Echlin. London: Novello and Company, Ltd., 1934.

Widor, Charles-Marie. _The Technique of the Modern Orchestra_, trans. Edward Suddard. London: Joseph Williams, Ltd., 1906.